Gift Baskets
How to Prepare Them

Gift Baskets
How to Prepare Them

Maureen Burgess

VNR VAN NOSTRAND REINHOLD COMPANY
New York Cincinnati Toronto London Melbourne

Copyright © 1983 by Van Nostrand Reinhold Company Inc.
Library of Congress Catalog Card Number 83-14673
ISBN 0-442-21323-9

Printed in the United States of America
Designed by Loudan Enterprises

Published by Van Nostrand Reinhold Company Inc.
135 West 50th Street
New York, New York 10020

Van Nostrand Reinhold Company Limited
Molly Millars Lane
Wokingham, Berkshire RG11 2PY, England

Van Nostrand Reinhold
480 La Trobe Street
Melbourne, Victoria 3000, Australia

Macmillan of Canada
Division of Gage Publishing Limited
164 Commander Boulevard
Agincourt, Ontario M1S 3C7, Canada

Library of Congress Cataloging in Publication Data

Burgess, Maureen.
    Making gift baskets.

    Includes index.
    1. Handicraft. 2. Baskets. 3. Gifts. I. Title.
    II. Title: Gift baskets.
TT157. B83 1984   745.5   83-14673
ISBN 0-442-21323-9

Contents

Part Three / Making Items for Baskets   67

Introduction

We have all been faced with the often difficult task of choosing gifts for family or friends. We want to give presents that are at once unique and useful. We flit from store to store, boutique to boutique, and counter to counter, unable to discover anything really special or different.

Often we spy something that we think has possibilities, only to discover shoddy workmanship or inferior materials. More often than not, we discover, too, that there are dozens of items around that are exactly the same: the next store we enter has the same thing in another color—hardly what one would call a special and unique gift! So, on our merry way we go, searching for "the" gift; ever hoping, but never finding it.

The answer to this problem is to be found in the world of gift baskets. Here one can find an unlimited source of gift ideas for mothers, fathers, children, relatives, friends, and even beloved pets.

Baskets are wonderful presents in and of themselves. Better yet, they can be filled with items specifically chosen just for a particular person—be he or she a cook, sportsman, gourmet, handyman, gardener, hobbyist, bride, mother-to-be, or eight-year-old. There truly is a basket for everyone.

I am going to show you how to make over a hundred different gift baskets, and you don't need any special education or dexterity in order to assemble these treasures. They are surprisingly easy to construct and will provide much pleasure and satisfaction for giver and receiver alike.

Part I of *Gift Baskets* will tell you about baskets themselves—how to buy them, how to line and decorate them, and finally, how to assemble the items within.

Part II presents dozens and dozens of basket projects, each one containing a list of items to include. There are gourmet baskets, tea baskets, fruit baskets, soap baskets, book baskets, get-well baskets, gardener's baskets, sewer's baskets, and a great many more. Specific instructions and possible options for the assembler are also provided.

Some of the items that fill the baskets can be bought, while others can be handmade at home. Part III contains directions for making a multitude of articles to add to your baskets—cheesecloth bags, sachets, lingerie cases, napkin holders, and pet toys are just a few. By making these items yourself, you can be sure of their quality and durability without putting a huge dent in your budget.

We give gifts to make other people happy, but actually we make ourselves happy in the process. Deciding exactly what would please Auntie, or Uncle, or dear old Mrs. So-and-So, who waters our plants while we are away, gives us a certain amount of anticipated pleasure. We take pride in wrapping and decorating the gift just so, knowing it will be appreciated. Nothing can compare with the excitement of presenting such a gift or with seeing the look of sheer delight on the person's face when he or she opens it.

Many people are under the mistaken impression that a gift has to be costly to mean anything. Nothing could be farther from the truth, and *Gift Baskets* will surely prove it to you. I believe most people would prefer a simple, honest token of friendship or love to an expensive, impersonal, assembly-line gift. In my opinion, there is no better way to express warm wishes for and thoughtfulness towards a person than to give a personalized basket containing the special things that person loves—gourmet delights, favorite wines and cheeses, a collection of exquisite sea shells, or knitting needles and yarns. If it makes *you* feel this good just to think about it, imagine how the recipient will feel when you present it.

Ideas for baskets are limited only by the interests of the person who is going to receive one and the basket maker's imagination. Use the suggestions in this book as a springboard. The possibilities are simply endless. You may never give another storebought gift again!

Part One

All About Baskets

DISCOVERING BASKETS

Maybe I should say "rediscovering baskets," since they have been around for quite some time—between 5,000 and 9,000 years. Basketmaking is one of the oldest crafts known to man: samples from prehistoric times have been found preserved in dry sand. Some of the ancient Egyptian basketmaking techniques are still being used today.

Baskets were used by ancient cultures in a variety of ways. Primitive people used them as household utensils for cooking and serving food. Baskets were also used as storage and carrying containers for food, clothing, and trinkets. Basketweaving was involved in the construction of houses and furnishings, shields and armor, and even musical instruments.

High-quality baskets have been found in some of the least developed areas of the world, and each culture has its own distinct and unique patterns. Indeed, one can tell where a basket was made and by whom just by looking at the design.

Figure I–1. Assorted Baskets

Today, baskets are becoming extremely popular once again. Large stores have sections devoted entirely to baskets of different shapes and sizes. Wicker boutiques are springing up all over the place; nearly every mall has one. There are even wicker warehouses—hundreds of square feet of floor space covered with wicker baskets, furniture, and wall-hangings.

If you have never been inside such a place, you are in for a very pleasant surprise. These shops are veritable paradises for basket lovers. Just be sure you have lots of will power (or plenty of spare cash) before you enter. One can get quite carried away buying this, that, and the other.

The individual basket is really very inexpensive, but if you have as little will power as I have (which happens to be none), you will choose at least half a dozen at a time. Then, there you are—arms loaded with baskets, finally on your way out of the shop—when your eye catches a little, oddly shaped basket you hadn't noticed earlier. Before you know it, you are back at the counter, having it wrapped. You feel a bit like someone cheating on a diet—marvelous but guilty.

You will find some very unusual shapes (octagonal, cylindrical, novelty) among the more basic ones (square, round, oblong, oval). Many baskets have lids, and some have handles or spaces where your fingers go for easy carrying. But no matter what the shape or size of the basket, an attractive gift can be made from it.

Baskets are so much more useful than cardboard boxes. They can be used over and over again, and because they are so attractive they do not have to be stashed away out of sight. They can be kept in view—on a table, on a shelf, or hung on the wall. Larger baskets can be used as containers and placed on the floor. Baskets can hold trinkets, candy, fruit, flowers, mail, bread, odds and ends, magazines, knitting, toys, vegetables, almost anything.

Baskets by themselves make wonderful gifts, but imagine one filled with fantastic things chosen just for you—a thoughtful, utterly charming present.

BUYING TIPS

Before you rush out to the nearest basket boutique, there are a few things you should have in mind.

• Look for quality workmanship. Avoid baskets with jagged edges or ends on the outside of the basket that might catch or break off. Any ends should be woven to the inside of the basket, as inconspicuously as possible, and smoothed so that they don't present sharp, dangerous areas that might cut skin or damage contents.
• Look for baskets that have good symmetry. Square baskets should be square and not pulled out of shape; round baskets should be round and not leaning towards oval; and so on.
• Try to buy baskets made entirely of natural materials. Plastic made to look like natural fiber somehow loses all its charm. Natural materials include wicker, willow, sisal, rushes, wool, raffia, grasses, jute, fabric, rope, reeds, bamboo, twine, wood, cane, and rattan.
• When purchasing a knitted or crocheted basket of any material, try to obtain one without visible knots or joins, at least in the middle of the basket. Unless the basket is very large, it should be constructed from a single roll of material with no distinct joins.
• If the basket you select has been painted, be sure it has been given a sufficient coat of paint to cover every inch—inside, outside, and between the woven pieces. If it was only given a quick once-over, it may have unpainted areas that give it a worn and shabby appearance. You could always repaint it yourself, but, after all, you are paying for a painted basket and not one you will have to touch up when you get home.
• Handles and lids should also be made of natural materials. Occasionally you may come across a lovely basket with synthetic handles or lid. Sometimes these are not particularly objectionable, but an all-natural basket looks so much better. Rather than settle for plastic, see if you can find baskets with wood or leather trimmings.

• Check the basket to see that it rests on its base firmly. If it is very wobbly or lopsided, look for another one.

• Perfection can be very boring and dull. Minor imperfections often add interest and appeal to an object, especially if it is a handcrafted item. You will have to be the judge in this case. Slight internal differences in texture, weaving materials, and color can give a basket individuality; a natural blemish or discoloration may add charm. However, do not mistake poor craftsmanship for originality—it just doesn't come off.

• It is a good idea to have at least an inkling of what you are looking for before you start out. It does simplify matters to know that you need, for example, a deep, square basket with a lid. In such a case, you can even phone first to get an idea of who stocks this particular type of basket.

• Have no qualms about buying baskets made outside your own country—provided, of course, that they are made from natural materials and not from synthetic imitations. Some of the loveliest baskets in the world come from Europe and the West Indies. If you vacation in areas that are famous for their baskets (Mexico, the Caribbean, the Orient), be sure to bring some back with you. They are usually very inexpensive and well constructed. You may find some quite colorful ones; others may have intricate designs woven throughout. American Indian baskets are particularly lovely. Oriental bazaars are good sources for baskets from China, Japan, Malaysia, and other exotic places.

• You may also care to look into the possibility of making your own baskets. This is a most rewarding hobby, giving much pleasure and satisfaction. It is beyond the scope of this book to explain how to weave your own baskets, but your local library will certainly have at least a few books on the subject. Two interesting titles you might look for are: *The Complete Book of Baskets and Basketry*, by Dorothy Wright (Scribner, 1978), and *Basketry Today with Materials from Nature*, by Dona Z. Meilach and Dee Menagh (Crown, 1979).

Read them thoroughly and then go to your neighborhood craft store for your materials and tools. You might purchase a kit to get yourself started, and then branch out from there. Making a basic basket is really quite uncomplicated. Start with a small basket and work up to bigger things; this way you will gain the confidence needed to undertake larger projects. If there is a school or craft shop near you that offers basket weaving among its courses, by all means sign up. You will learn a fine old craft and meet new people. The cost is usually minimal.

PREPARING BASKETS

Now that you have purchased your basket (or baskets, as the case may be) you have two choices: you can leave the baskets as is; or you can decorate them and make them look more festive by adding a colorful lining, some pretty bows, or even some paint.

Should you decide to leave the baskets as is, all you have to do is dust them and fill them with gifts. For dusting, use the small brush attachment on your vacuum cleaner or a clean, soft-bristled brush of some kind. You may also slip baskets under the shower for a few seconds for a quick washing, and then let them dry thoroughly before filling.

Painting Baskets

Although I think a natural basket has much more charm than a painted one, I sometimes succumb to my whims and paint a small one to produce a certain effect.

Since paint has a tendency to flake off of baskets, it is not a good idea to paint baskets that will be used frequently (such as shopping baskets or clothes baskets). Paint only ones that will be used mainly for ornamental purposes—as a hair clip holder, vanity tray, or candy dish, for example.

To paint a basket, follow these simple steps:

1. Clean

Always start with a clean basket. Brush away any dust, then wash the basket with warm water, if necessary, and dry thoroughly.

2. Seal

Seal the basket with a light coat of white shellac, varnish, or Podgy or Mod Podge (a thick, opaque white mixture used for gluing, sealing, and glazing—available at most craft stores).

3. Paint

Spray on one or two coats of the selected paint or apply the paint with a good-quality paint brush. If you decide to spray, be sure you work in a well-ventilated room and wear a spraying mask. Ideally, spraying would be done outside. Place the basket in a large cardboard box and use this as your spraying "room." Spray the basket upright; then turn it over and spray the underside. Make sure the basket is completely covered with paint—inside, outside, and between the woven material. Let the paint dry thoroughly, and then inspect the basket; respray, if you think it is necessary to do so.

If you use a brush, apply the paint with the same thoroughness you would use if spraying, being sure to cover the whole basket, inside and out. Don't put the paint on too thickly: you are much better off with two very light coats than with one thick, messy one. The baskets do not need lots of paint, just enough to give them color.

Be sure to let the baskets dry thoroughly. Paint them a couple of days before you need them so that the paint will have time to "set." Use acrylic paint, spray lacquer, or oil-based paint, and a good-quality brush with synthetic bristles.

4. Glaze

After the paint is good and dry, apply a thin coat of glazing material. Use white shellac, varnish, or Podgy, or use a liquid plastic—one with either a high-gloss finish or a matte, satin finish. When this coating has dried, you can fill your baskets to your liking.

Lining Baskets

Lining a basket with some pretty fabric makes it look very festive and adds that little extra touch. A multitude of fabrics can be used, including gingham, calico, velvet, cotton, duck, denim, linen, fake fur, felt, organdy, burlap, and satin.

All you need to make your lining is a paper pattern of your basket. To produce this pattern, you will need the following items:

Tape Measure	Scissors
Pencil	Tissue Paper
Ruler	Compass (for circular baskets)

Now simply follow these steps:

1. Measure the Basket

For square or rectangular baskets, measure the length and width of the basket bottom and add $\frac{1}{2}$" all around. Measure the length of each side and add 1". Measure the depth of each side and add $1\frac{1}{2}$". Transfer these measurements to paper and cut out the pattern. See Figure I-2. For round baskets, measure the diameter of the basket bottom and add 1". Measure the *inside* circumference at the top of the basket and add 1"; then measure the depth of the basket and add $1\frac{1}{2}$". This will give you the side measurement. Transfer these measurements to paper and cut out the pattern. See Figure I-3. If the basket has sloping sides, so that the bottom is smaller than the top, simply cut the pattern to the above measurements, anyway; the lower edge can then be gathered to fit the bottom basket piece, giving a custom-fitted lining. See Figure I-4.

2. Construct the Lining

Linings can be sewn together by hand or machine. Working by hand has a certain advantage over machine stitching—you can take your project with you and work on it during your lunch break or during any spare time you happen to have (while waiting in a doctor's office or a dentist's waiting room, for example).

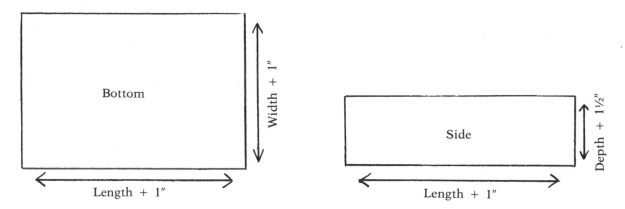

Figure I–2. Lining Baskets: How to measure square and rectangular baskets.

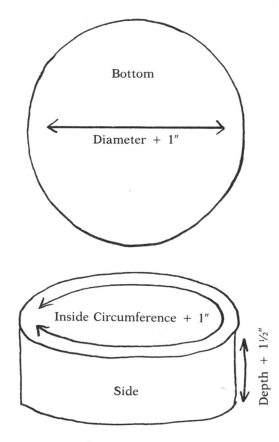

Figure I–3. Lining Baskets: How to measure round baskets.

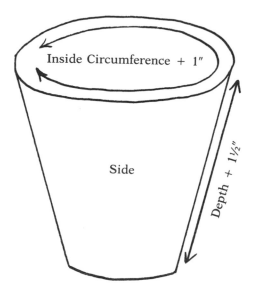

Figure I–4. Lining Baskets: How to measure baskets with sloping sides.

3. Make the Lining

For all linings, stay stitch around each piece of lining as follows: using regular machine stitch, sew all around the lining pieces, $\frac{1}{2}''$ in from their edges. Refer to Figures I-5 through I-8 and to the Machine and Hand Stitch Guides, and follow one of these methods:

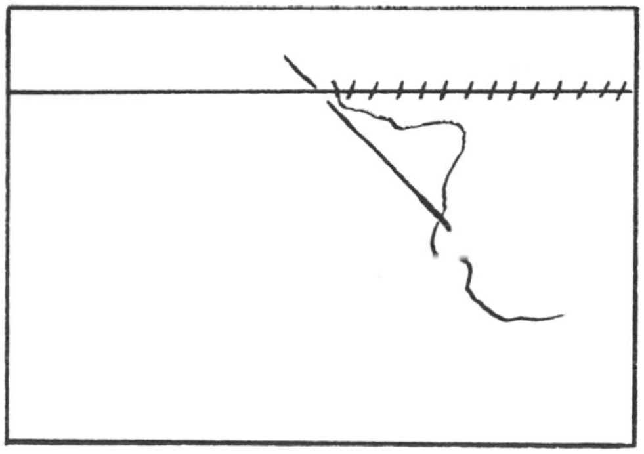

Method #1 for Square or Rectangular Linings

Join the side piece at its short ends, right sides together, using $\frac{1}{2}''$ seams and regular machine stitch. Press all the seams open. See Figure I-9. Pin the side piece to the bottom piece, right sides together. Clip the material down to the stay stitching at the corners of the side piece for ease

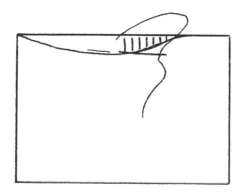

Figure I–5. Hand Hem Stitch: Take tiny stitches along the folded edge of the fabric. Pick up the fabric only a few threads at a time. Hem stitches are used to finish the top edge of a lining.

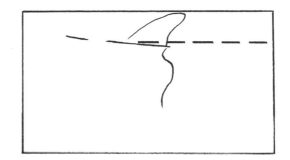

Figure I–7. Hand Basting: All basting stitches are large stitches. Pick up a small amount of fabric and pull the thread through; then reinsert the needle $\frac{1}{4}''-\frac{1}{2}''$ farther along and take another stitch about $\frac{1}{4}''-\frac{1}{2}''$ wide. Repeat in this manner all along the row. Basting is used to make gathers.

Figure I–6. Hand Blind Stitch: Pick up a small amount of fabric on the inside of the seam line on one side of the closing; then pull the thread through. Take another stitch the same way on the opposite side. Continue in this manner all along the closing. Pull the threads gently as you go along to form an invisible seam. Blind stitches are used to join the top of a double lining.

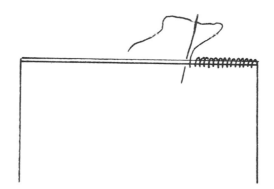

Figure I–8. Hand Overstitch: Take small stitches over and over along the top or along the edges of seams. Overstitching is used to construct seams for cardboard linings.

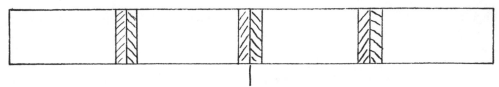

Seams Pressed Open

Figure I–9. Method #1 for sewing square or rectangular linings.

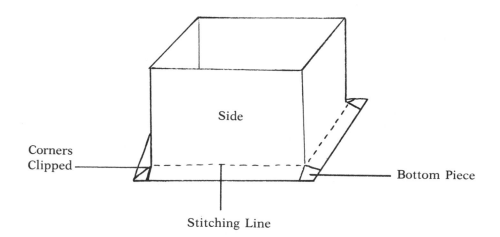

Corners Clipped

Side

Bottom Piece

Stitching Line

Figure I–10. Method #1 for sewing square or rectangular linings.

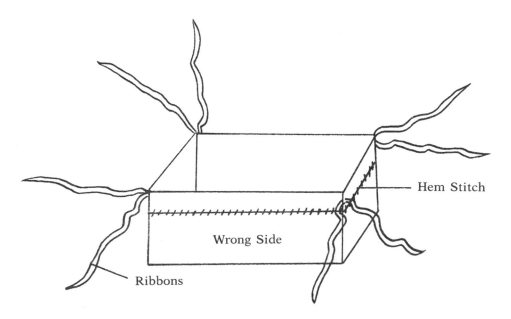

Hem Stitch

Wrong Side

Ribbons

Figure I–11. Method #1 for sewing square or rectangular linings.

in placing. Stitch all around, $\frac{1}{2}''$ in from the edges, using regular machine stitch. See Figure I-10.

Fold the material under, $\frac{1}{2}''$ along the top edge, and press. Fold under another $\frac{1}{2}''$, and press. Stitch close to the edge all around the top, by machine or by hand. See Figure I-11.

Fold a 20'' piece of ribbon in half and stitch through the center of it to each corner of the lining, on the wrong side, as in Figure I-11. Cut the ends of the ribbon on the diagonal.

Place the lining in the basket, right side out, and pull the ribbons through woven canes to the outside of the basket. Tie the ribbon in bows.

Method #2 for Square or Rectangular Linings

This method calls for thin cardboard and polyester-type quilt batting. Batting can be bought at craft or fabric stores. First, cut the lining pieces from the fabric. Next, cut the thin cardboard the *exact* size of the basket bottom and sides; then cut the batting pieces to match the cardboard.

Using white glue, attach the batting to one side of the corresponding pieces of cardboard. Let this dry. Place the cardboard, batting side down, on the wrong side of the corresponding lining fabric. Apply glue to the back of the cardboard, along the edges only, and then press the excess fabric over and down onto the glued surface. Weight this down with a book or something similar until the glue has dried.

Cut a piece of fabric or felt to fit the back of the cardboard, spread glue over the surface of the cardboard, and press onto it the fabric or felt. Let this dry.

To assemble the lining, place the side pieces right sides together (the padded surface is the right side) and overstitch the seams. Overstitch the side piece to the bottom piece. See Figure I-12. Attach ribbons as you would in method #1.

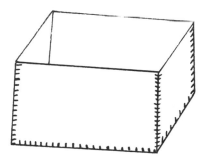

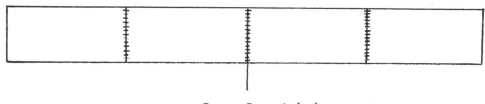

Seams Overstitched

Figure I–12. Method #2 for sewing square or rectangular linings.

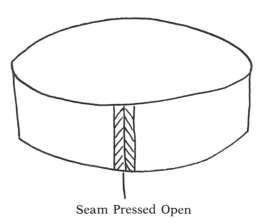

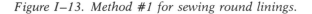

Seam Pressed Open

Figure I–13. Method #1 for sewing round linings.

Method #1 for Round Linings

Join the side piece at its short ends, right sides together, using a ½″ seam and regular machine stitch. Press open. See Figure I-13. Pin the side piece to the bottom piece, right sides together, clipping the material down to the stay stitching every inch or so for ease in placing. Stitch all around, ½″ in from the edges, with regular machine stitch. See Figure I-14. Finish the top of the lining as you would a square lining, sewing ribbons an equal distance from each other as shown in Figure I-14.

Instead of using ribbons, you may use ordinary white glue daubed here and there along the inside top of the basket to secure the lining. This is ideal for baskets you do not wish to put bows on.

Method #2 for Round Linings

Make two identical linings, and tuck one inside the other, wrong sides together. Blind stitch along the top edge and attach the ribbons. This lining has a little more body to it.

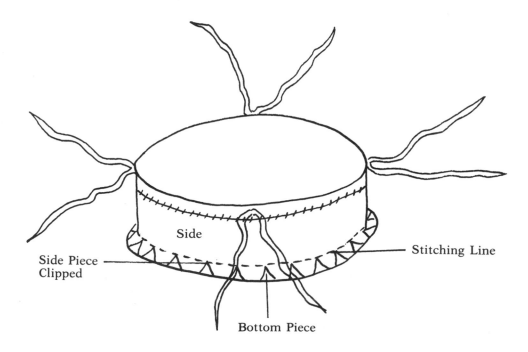

Side

Stitching Line

Side Piece Clipped

Bottom Piece

Figure I–14. Method # 1 for sewing round linings.

Method for Round Basket with Sloping Sides

Join the side piece at its short ends as you would in method #1 for regular round linings. Press the seam open. Using a basting stitch, stitch all around the bottom edge, ½″ from the edges. Baste again, ¼″ in from edge. You now have two rows of stitching. See Figure I-15. Gather the side piece gently by pulling the basting threads, one thread from each row simultaneously, until the piece fits the bottom piece. See Figure I-16. Anchor the threads around a pin. Pin the gathered edge to the bottom piece, right sides together, adjusting the gathers evenly. Stitch all around with regular machine stitch, ½″ in from edge. Finish the top as you would in method #1 for regular round linings.

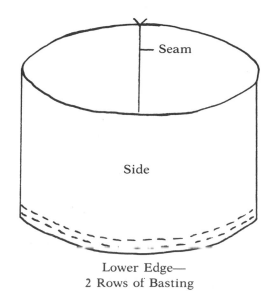

Lower Edge—
2 Rows of Basting

Figure I–15. Method for sewing linings for round baskets with sloping sides.

Machine Stitch Guide

Fabric	Stitches Per Inch	Needle	Thread
Sheer	16–20	Fine #9	75–150
Light	12–16	Fine #11	60–75
Medium	10–12	Med. #14	50–60
Heavy	8–10	Med.–Coarse #14–#18	8–36
Very Heavy	6–8	Med.–Coarse #14–#18	8–36

Regular machine stitch—12 stitches to the inch.
Maching basting—6 stitches to the inch.
Use Mercerized thread on sheer, light, and medium fabrics. Use heavy-duty Mercerized thread on heavy or very heavy fabrics. Use nylon or polyester thread on all synthetics.

Hand Stitch Guide

Fabric	Needle
Sheer	#9, #10
Light	#8, #9
Medium	#6, #7, #8
Heavy	#4, #5
Very Heavy	#1–#5

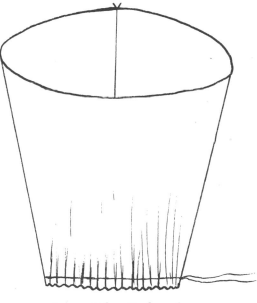

Lower Edge Gathered

Figure I–16. Method for sewing linings for round baskets with sloping sides.

Adding Finishing Touches

You may "finish" your basket by adding a row of piping in a matching or contrasting color around the top edge of the lining or by making some fabric bows. The bows can then be tied on each side of a handle, or around the sides of the basket, or wherever you want them. Ribbons can also be twined around basket handles and tied in bows on either side at the base.

Piping

You can buy ready-made piping, or you can make your own. To make your own, purchase enough preshrunk piping cord to go all around the top of your lining, with 1" to spare. Use heavy cord for heavy or very heavy fabrics and finer cord for lighter fabrics. Cover the cord with bias strips. To make bias strips, fold a corner of the fabric so that crosswise threads are parallel to the lengthwise threads; then cut along the fold line. See Figure I-17. Cut strips that are about 1½" wide. Join the strips, right sides together, so that their lengthwise threads are parallel. Use regular machine stitch and ½" seams. See Figure I-18. Trim the seams and press them open. Join as many strips as you will need to cover the length of your piping cord, plus 1". Join the ends of the strips to form a continuous band.

Fray both ends of the piping cord for about ½". Join the ends by overlapping and securing them with a drop of glue. Fold the bias strip over the cord, with the right side of the fabric out, and stitch all around, close to the cord. Use the piping or zipper foot attachment on your machine.

Pin the piping to the wrong side of the top edge of the lining. Blind stitch it into place. If you are using a double lining, insert the piping before sewing the two linings together.

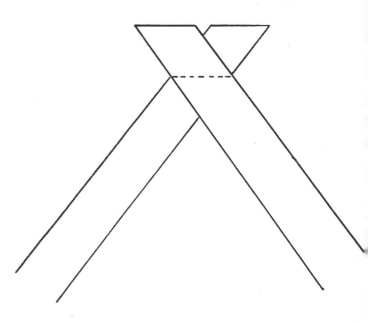

Figure I–17. Making bias strips.

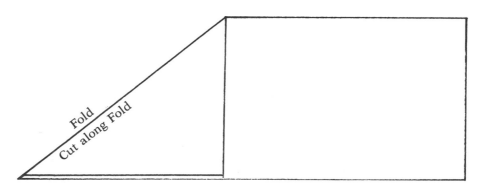

Figure I–18. Joining bias strips.

Fabric Bows

Cut two pieces of fabric for each bow. For a small basket, cut each piece 18″ × 1″. For a medium-sized basket, cut each piece 20″ × 1½″. For a large basket, cut each piece 24″ × 2″. Cut the short ends on the diagonal. See Figure I-19.

Place the pieces right sides together, pin them and stitch along one long side and the two short ends, using regular machine stitch. Sew ½″ in from the edges. On the other long side, stitch in from each corner, leaving a 6″ opening in the center. Trim off the corners just above the stitching. See Figure I-20. Turn the bow right side out through the opening. Push out the points of the corners with scissors or a wooden pick. Press the bow and blind stitch across the opening.

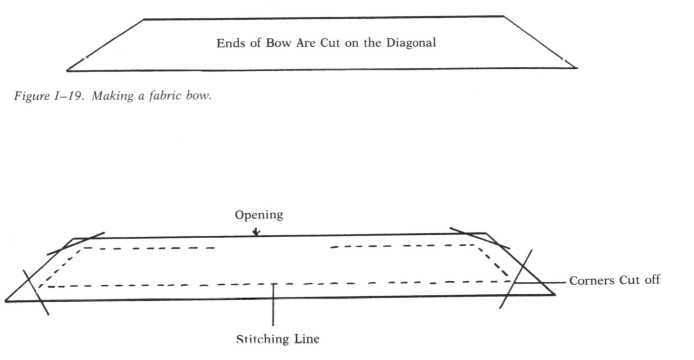

Ends of Bow Are Cut on the Diagonal

Figure I–19. Making a fabric bow.

Opening

Corners Cut off

Stitching Line

Figure I–20. On the other long side of the bow, stitch in from each corner.

Fillings for Baskets

Baskets that are not fabric-lined can be filled with shredded cellophane, parchment excelsior, tissue paper, or crepe paper.

Shredded Cellophane

Shredded cellophane is an attractive, fluffy packing material. It is usually found in more expensive gifts or small beauty items, such as scented soaps or bath cubes. You may find little packages of this material in dime stores at Easter time. Easter colors are usually limited to pink, green, yellow, and mauve, but these look delightful in food, baby, or women's specialty baskets.

Cellophane is best suited to small or medium baskets because it is more costly than other fillings and because it tends to settle after awhile, requiring you to be very generous when filling your basket with it. Colors most readily available are gold, red, green, and the Easter colors mentioned above. Look for cellophane at your local craft or gift store. If you cannot find it there, try contacting a florist or gift wholesaler.

Parchment Excelsior

Parchment excelsior is a slightly harder material than cellophane. It does not settle quite as much as cellophane does, and, being somewhat firmer, it offers more support to the gift items—making it ideal for larger baskets.

You probably will not find this material readily in stores; you might have to contact a paper supplier. However, you may have some luck, as I did, and find a friendly merchant who will give you all the excelsior his products come packaged in. It is usually only thrown away, so be brave and ask around at gift shops, jewelry stores, and fruit stands for their discards. They will probably be happy to have you take it away.

Tissue or Crepe Paper

Tissue or crepe paper is only suitable for small or medium-sized baskets, since it is uneconomical for larger ones. This material can be found in most craft and gift shops and comes in many different colors—blue, pink, red, purple, green, yellow, white, orange. You may also come across gold or silver.

This material should be gently crumpled before being placed in the basket. Heavy items will crush it, so you will have to pack your basket according to the weight of the items.

If you wish to pack a large basket with some pretty-colored bedding, try filling it first with parchment excelsior and then adding a layer of crumpled tissue paper in the chosen color. Its appearance will be just as effective, and the arrangement will not cost as much as using all tissue. Cellophane can also be placed on top of a bed of excelsior.

Whatever packing material you choose for your baskets, be generous with it. You should be able to see it among the gift items.

ARRANGING BASKETS

When designing your baskets, there are a few things you should keep in mind.

• The basket, lining or packing material, gift items, and wrap should all harmonize nicely. A large basket that was lined with a nautical-patterned terrycloth lining and held small jars of honey or slabs of cheese would look odd to say the least. It is far more appropriate to fill this type of basket with beach items and to place the honeys or cheeses in a smaller basket on gold shredded cellophane.
• Consider the size of the basket in relation to the gift items. Small items should be in small baskets, large items in larger baskets. If the size of the basket is out of proportion to the gift items, it will spoil the overall appearance.
• Be selective when adding bows. They look lovely on food, baby, or beauty baskets, but are out of place on men's, beach, or garden baskets, for instance. These baskets look better plain than all gussied up.
• Try to arrange the items in the baskets, rather than just tossing them in haphazardly. Place small items at the front and space the items evenly.

Figure I–21. Using colored cellophane to wrap a basket.

Be sure to nestle them down in the bedding material instead of perching them on top of it. Items should look "comfortable" and "at home" in their baskets, not as though just temporarily residing there.

• Don't overload baskets. This is the final temptation to overcome: it is not necessary to cram in absolutely everything. A few items will make an attractive basic basket. If instead you include too many items, the beauty of the basket will be hidden. A few well-chosen articles arranged decoratively look so much more appealing.

For example, consider a basic wine basket, consisting of 2 sparkling wine glasses, 1 bottle of red wine, and a corkscrew. As options, you could complement or replace one of more of the original items with 1 bottle of white wine, 1 bottle of champagne, 1 or 2 slabs of cheese, 1 or 2 boxes of gourmet crackers, or a book about wines. Decorate the basket with a few silk flowers, and you will have a wonderful gift basket.

Keep in mind that the more items you include, the larger the basket ought to be. If you decide on a small basic basket, but later change your mind about the number or size of the gift items, change the size of the basket too.

• The shape of the basket isn't hugely important. You can use any shape for any gift. However, some items do look better in certain shapes. For example, long, thin baskets are best suited to long, thin items such as candles, utensils, and knives. For most of your gifts, choose shallow baskets: these require less filling material. Save the deeper baskets for items like bottles or rolled towels that can be stood up on end.

There are many different novelty-shaped baskets on the market—chickens, rabbits, fish, frogs. These would make wonderful children's or infant's baskets.

• Put your imagination to work when designing your gifts. Tuck a few silk flowers or butterflies here and there for a touch of elegance. Add a little fake fur mouse to a cheese basket, a pair of ear muffs to a baby basket, a favorite cold remedy to a winter treats basket, a small ice bag to a bartender's basket, or some tiny chenille bees to a honey basket.

Not only does this add a bit of humor, but you will find that these things "complete" your basket and pull everything together.

WRAPPING BASKETS

Actually, wrapping is the most difficult part of making a gift basket, since some baskets can be rather awkward to wrap.

The best material for wrapping baskets is colored cellophane. It is not too easy to find, but you may have some luck at your local craft store or paper supplier. Other possible materials are tissue paper, fabric, gift wrap, and clear plastic bags.

Small baskets present no problems. They can be slipped into a cellophane bag or placed on a square of wrap. The top edges are then gathered together and secured with an elastic band. A length of ribbon is tied around the elastic in a bow. A square of fabric, cut with pinking shears, can be used the same way, but spray the square with starch first, heavily at the outer edges.

Larger baskets can of course be treated in the same manner, if you can find wrap big enough. However, if you have a really large basket that refuses to fit your largest piece of wrap, just add a large bow and give it as is. If you want the contents of the basket to be a surprise, tuck a few sheets of tissue paper loosely over the top of the gift.

Part Two

A Portfolio of Baskets

On the following pages you will find ideas for many different baskets—something for everyone. You needn't feel bound by these, however. You can easily make up your own once you get the hang of it.

All you have to do is think about the person you wish to give the basket to. What kind of person is he or she? Is he/she the outdoor or indoor type? What sort of hobbies, interests or talents does he/she have? Is he/she moving to a new house? Is he/she a collector? Find out as much as you can about the person and then make up a basket especially for him or her.

This way you will come up with a very personal gift. It will be suitable only for the person you are giving it to—a unique present, spilling over with love and thoughtfulness.

GOURMET BASKETS

Gourmet baskets are my favorite kind of gift basket. The world of good food has so much to offer, and just about everyone likes to eat.

What better way is there to introduce friends to exotic cuisines than with a lovely basket filled with wonderfully delicious treats from other lands. A basket filled with bread ingredients would soon be responsible for delightful aromas wafting from a friend's kitchen. Or how about a basket of fragrant honeys, or pungent spices, or polished fruit, or maybe aromatic herbs?

I could go on and on, and actually I did have quite a time deciding what gourmet selections to include in this section. I could easily have made up a list the size of all the baskets in this book, filled exclusively with food products.

These baskets look especially appealing if the items they contain are nestled in excelsior or shredded cellophane. If you like a certain food but not its container, consider transferring the contents to a glass jar, pretty box, or cellophane bag. Just add a ribbon or bow and an identification tag, and you are all set.

Take advantage of food items you can purchase in bulk form. Buy small amounts and package them yourself in little plastic bags or in fabric bags you make at home.

Baskets of this sort make ideal bon-voyage, shower, welcome-home, housewarming and thank-you gifts.

Herb Basket

Herb Basket

You may buy the herbs in small glass jars, or purchase them in bulk form and make up your own little packets. Attach a label to each packet and tie the packet with a little bow; then pile them into the basket.

Herbs You Might Include:

Basil	Lovage
Bay	Marjoram
Borage	Mint
Camomile	Oregano
Chives	Parsley
Chervil	Rosemary
Dill	Sage
Fennel	Salad Burnet
Garlic	Savory
Garlic Powder	Tarragon
Lemon Balm	Thyme

Options:
A Book about Herbs
A Herbal Cookbook

Bouquet Garni Basket

Bouquet garni consists of three or four herbs tied together in a little bag. This assortment is used for flavoring stews, soups, and sauces.

Bouquet Garni:

3 sprigs Parsley	$\frac{1}{4}$ tsp Thyme
1 Bay Leaf	6 Celery Leaves

Wrap all the ingredients in a small cheesecloth bag (see Part III of this book). Tie the bag with a long thread. The bag is removed from food before serving.

Bags may be put in the basket loose or piled in a small decorative glass container.

Options:
Recipe Book for Stews and Soups
Favorite Recipes of Your Own

Bouquet Garni Basket

Fines Herbes Basket

This blend of fine herbs is used in egg, cheese, and fish dishes.

Fines Herbes:

Chervil	Tarragon
Parsley	Chives

Place 1 or 1½ tsp of equal amounts of the above ingredients in a small cheesecloth bag (see Part III of this book); tie with a long thread. Herbs may be sprinkled on some dishes, such as omelets and baked fish.

Options:
Cookbook
Favorite Recipes

Spice Basket

Again, buy the spices in tiny glass jars or in bulk and make up your own bags. This basket is highly aromatic, a most delightful gift.

Spices You Might Include:

Allspice	Cumin
Anise	Curry
Cardamom	Ginger
Caraway	Mace
Chili Powder	Nutmeg
Cinnamon	Paprika
Cloves	Tamarind
Coriander	Turmeric

Options:
Book about Spices
Favorite Recipes
Book on Cooking with Spices

Seasonings Basket

No self-respecting cook would use anything but freshly ground seasonings. Indeed, a serious gourmet would become quite indignant if offered anything else.

Seasonings Basket

You will find some rather attractive plastic or ceramic salt and pepper mills on the market now, as well as the popular wooden ones. Some are quite decorative, with hand-painted floral or oriental designs.

Seasoning Items You Might Include:

Salt and Pepper Set	White Peppercorns
Black Peppercorns	Salt

Vinegar Basket

If you think vinegar comes in only one form—white—you are in for a nice surprise. There are many varieties, each having a distinct flavor all its own. Try some of the herbal vinegars yourself and have a taste treat you never had before.

You will probably have to visit a gourmet specialty shop or department to find most of these vinegars. However, you should be able to get at least five kinds at your supermarket.

Stand the vinegars up in a deep basket or lay them side by side in a shallow one.

Vinegars You Might Include:

Red Wine	White
White Wine	Malt
Sherry Wine	Cider
Rice Wine	Fruit
Garlic	Herbal

Options:
Vinegar Cruet
Book about Vinegars

Mustard Basket

Mustard is mustard—right? Wrong. There are many different kinds of mustard, ranging from very mild to extra hot. Gourmet shops are the most likely places in which to find all the varieties.

Arrange a few jars of gourmet mustards on a bed of gold or green shredded cellophane or crumpled tissue paper.

Mustards You Might Include:

Dijon	Poupon
Herb-Flavored	Wine-Flavored
Dry Mustard	Imported Mustards

Options:

Tiny Mustard Jars
Mustard Spoons
Recipes

Condiment Basket

Condiments complement other foods. Examples are: mint sauce with roast lamb, applesauce with pork chops, and horseradish or crabapples with roast beef. You can find most of these items in the supermarket. Arrange you choice of items on a bed of colored cellophane.

Condiments You Might Include:

Horseradish	Chutney
Mustard	Mint Sauce
Spiced Crabapples	Applesauce
Sweet Pickles	Gherkins
Dill Pickles	Mustard Pickles
Pickled Onions	Pickled Beets
Cranberry Sauce	Kumquats

Options:

Pickle Forks
Fancy Toothpicks
Small Condiment Dishes

Mustard Basket

Cooking Wine Basket

Cooking Wine Basket

A very attractive yet inexpensive gift can be made by purchasing bottles of cooking wines from your local supermarket. Arrange them on tissue paper or cellophane and add a few silk flowers.

Wines You Might Include:

Red Wine	Sherry
White Wine	Brandy

Options:
Glass Measuring Cup
Cooking with Wine Book

Tea Basket

A steaming cup of fragrant herbal tea is most delightful and refreshingly delicious. Introduce your friends to the marvelous assortment of teas and herbal blends available now, with such irresistible names as Lemon Mist, Mandarin Orange

Tea Basket

Spice, Red Zinger, Sleepy Time, Country Apple, and Cinnamon Rose. They are available at health food stores and some supermarkets.

Teas You Might Include:

Jasmine	Lemon
Mint	Green
Herbal	Earl Grey
Darjeeling	Breakfast
Orange Pekoe	Souchong

Options:
Small China Teapot
Cup(s) and Saucer(s)
Tea Cozy
Small Jar of Honey
Small Milk and Sugar Containers

Coffee Basket

This makes an ideal gift for a true coffee fanatic. He or she can lovingly grind his or her own coffee beans and even blend coffee beans for different flavors.

Items You Might Include:

Small Coffee Grinder	Coffee Measure
Small Bags of Gourmet	Coffee Spoons
Coffee Beans	Filters

Options:
Book about Coffee
Coffee Cookbook
Fancy Coffee Cup(s) and Saucer(s)

Drinking Wine Basket

This basket makes a lovely anniversary or housewarming present. Arrange the items on colored tissue paper or parchment excelsior.

Items You Might Include:
2 Wine Glasses
Corkscrew
Bottle of Red Wine

Options:
Bottle of White Wine
Bottle of Champagne
Book on Wines
1 or 2 Slabs of Cheese
1 or 2 Boxes of Gourmet Crackers

Mulled Wine Basket

Mulled wine makes an enticing gift for the winter holidays. Arrange the ingredients on crumpled brown tissue paper.

Ingredients:

Bottle of Red, White, or Rosé Wine	Whole Cloves
Small Bag of Sugar	Lemons
Stick Cinnamon	Oranges

Options:
Wine Glasses
Cheeses

You might also include the following simple recipe with the basket:

Mulled Wine Recipe:

1 bottle Red Wine	$\frac{1}{2}$ tsp Lemon Peel
$\frac{1}{4}$ cup Sugar	$\frac{1}{2}$ tsp Orange Peel
$2\frac{1}{2}$–3 inches Stick Cinnamon	6–8 Whole Cloves

Simmer all ingredients gently for 5–6 min. Strain and serve hot with thin slices of orange floating on top. Serves about 8.

Drinking Wine Basket

Seed and Nut Basket

Buy shelled or unshelled seeds and nuts. Make little burlap bags and fill them with unshelled nuts; then tie with colored cord or ribbon. Put shelled nuts and seeds in small cellophane bags and tie as above.

Seeds and Nuts You Might Include:

Pecans	Chestnuts
Almonds	Peanuts
Walnuts	Hazelnuts
Brazils	Pistachios
Cashews	Pumpkin Seeds
Sunflower Seeds	Sesame Seeds

Liqueur Basket

Liqueur Basket

This basket will be hard to fill only because of the wide variety of delicious liqueurs to choose from.

Liqueurs You Might Include:

Banana	Strawberry
Black Currant	Chocolate
Praline	Herbal
Apricot	Pear
Peppermint	Cherry
Chocolate Mint	Raspberry
Almond	Orange
Plum	Melon

Options:
2–4 Liqueur Glasses
Small Glass Tray

Honey Basket

If you can find yellow or orange shredded cellophane, use it for the bedding in your basket. It looks beautiful under jars of golden honey.

Honeys You Might Include:

Orange Blossom	Linden Blossom
Goldenrod	Clover
Comb Honey	Creamed Honey
Alfalfa	Heather
Sage	Buckwheat
Lavender	Tupelo
Wildflower	Blueberry

Options:
Honey Dipper
Book about Honey

Dried Fruit Basket

Candied fruit can also be added to this basket, along with candied peel, making a very colorful basket. Package dried fruit in cellophane bags, tie with ribbon (tightly), and arrange in basket.

Dried or Candied Fruits You Might Include:

Apricots	Apples
Dates	Prunes
Pineapples	Raisins
Bananas	Currants
Figs	Papayas
Any Candied Peels	

Options:
Cookbook Using Dried Fruits
Book on How to Dry Your Own Foods

Soup Mix Basket

Buy soup mix ingredients in bulk and make up little cellophane bags of them. Be sure to obtain the directions for making up the soup. Take a notebook and pencil to the store with you and copy down the instructions.

Honey Basket

Soup Ingredients You Might Include:

Assorted Soup Mixes	Bag of Rice
Bag of Noodles	Bag of Barley
Bay Leaves	Lentils
Dried Vegetables	Split Peas

Options:
Book on Homemade Soups
Box of Croutons
Bread Sticks

Health Food Basket

This is a fascinating basket to put together, especially if you buy everything in bulk and make up individual bags at home. You will find all of the items listed here at health food or specialty shops and at supermarkets.

Baskets lined with brown and beige country print fabric and decorated with brown satin bows harmonize nicely with these wholesome foods.

Health Food Basket

Health Foods You Might Include:

Skim Milk Powder	Oatmeal
Bran	Wheat Germ
Sesame Seeds	Brown Rice
Cereal Grains	Nuts
Seeds	Dried Fruit
Corn Meal	Corn Starch
Raisins	Honey
Granola	Herb Teas

Options:
Book on Nutrition
Natural Foods Cookbook

Bread Basket

In this basket, include everything one would need to make a delicious loaf of bread. You will probably need a fairly large basket for this gift. Use some pretty calico or country print fabric for a lining.

Ingredients:

Unbleached Hard	Yeast
Wheat Flour	Rye Flour
Whole Wheat Flour	Sugar
Milk Powder	Bran
Wheat Germ	Raisins
Corn Meal	Nuts
Vegetable Oil	Herbs
Wheat Berries	Honey

Options:
Book on Bread Making
Bread Pans
Wooden Spoons
Large Mixing Bowl (used as basket)

Cheese Basket

There are so many different cheeses on the store shelves that it makes choosing very difficult. I would suggest first buying a mild, a medium, and a strong cheese, and then add varieties as you wish.

Cheeses You Might Include:

Mild	*Medium*	*Strong*
Brick	Brie	Cheddar
Camembert	Herb Cheeses	Cheshire
Mozzerella	Swiss	Blue
Edam	Havarti	Gorgonzola
Monterey Jack	Colby	Limburger
Muenster	Cheddar	Feta

Options:
Cheeseboard and Knife
Cheese Cutter
Bottle of Wine
Gourmet Crackers
Book about Cheeses
Fruit—Pears or Apples
Cheese Cookbook

Italian Food Basket

Not many people can resist the marvelous dishes of Italy—tender pasta, aromatic herbs, delicious cheeses, and tangy tomato sauces. Pile all the things you choose into a large basket and listen to all the oohs and ahs.

Italian Food Ingredients You Might Include:

Assorted Pasta Shapes	Grated Parmesan
Tomato Sauce	Cheese
Tomato Paste	Grated Romano
Pepperoni Sausage	Cheese
Herbs—Parsley, Basil,	Olive Oil
Oregano, Garlic	

Options:
Pizza Cutter
Spaghetti Stirrer
Red Wine
Italian Cookbook

Italian Food Basket

Chinese Food Basket

You could use a metal wok or a large bamboo steamer as the "basket." You would probably be quite surprised at how many people eat Chinese food. This method of cooking food has become extremely popular.

Chinese Food Ingredients You Might Include:

Ginger Root	Garlic
Light Soy Sauce	Water Chestnuts
Corn Starch	Sherry
Oyster Sauce	Chinese Cookbook
Chinese Noodles	

Options.
Chinese Cleaver
Rice Bowls
Chinese Utensils
Chopsticks

Salad Basket

Salad Basket

Almost everyone loves a cool, crisp, fresh green salad, all crunchy and flavorful with a wonderful homemade dressing.

Salad Ingredients You Might Include:

Lemon Juice	Garlic
Olive Oil	Dry Mustard
Vinegars	Croutons
Salad Herbs—Basil,	Worcestershire
Chervil, Dill, Mint,	Sauce
Tarragon, Parsley	

Options:
Small Wooden Salad Bowls
Salad Dressing Server
Salad Servers
Vegetable Peeler
Salad Dryer
Dressing Recipes
Book about Making Salads
Large Wooden Salad Bowl (used as basket)

Chinese Food Basket

Groceries Basket

This basket makes a good shower or house-warming gift. A deep basket looks best, lined with some country print cotton fabric.

Groceries You Might Include:

All-Purpose Flour	Salt
Baking Powder	Pepper
Baking Soda	Mustard
Corn Starch	Vinegar
Pasta	Tomato Sauce
Rice	Steak Sauce
Noodles	Worcestershire Sauce
Tabasco	Barbecue Sauce
Beef Consummé	Chicken Broth

Options:
Book on Nutrition
Cookbook

Homemade Goodies Basket

If you are handy in the kitchen and make your own jams, jellies, marmalades, pickles, chutneys, you have the makings of a really lovely gift. In today's world, where just about everything you eat is loaded with fillers and chemical additives of some sort, it is a treat to taste homemade goodness.

Homemade Items You Might Include:

Jams	Jellies
Pickles	Chutneys
Cookies	Fruit Cake
Marmalades	Candy
Canned Fruit	Mustard

Options:
Small, Fancy Serving Dishes
Jam Spoons
Pickle Forks
Favorite Recipes

Fresh Fruit Basket

This basket will have to be made up almost at the time you are going to give it. However, this doesn't usually cause any problems.

Use only fresh, unblemished fruit of any sort that will last a few days.

Polish smooth-skinned fruit until shiny. Wipe citrus fruit just until clean. Arrange the fruit on a bed of shredded cellophane or tissue paper. Combine more than one kind of fruit in a basket if you wish or simply stick with all one sort.

Fresh Fruits You Might Include:

Apples	Oranges
Limes	Lemons
Tangerines	Plums
Mandarin Oranges	Grapefruit
Pears	Pomegranates

Options:
Fruit Dishes
Fruit Knives and Spoons

Sprout Basket

Give someone fresh sprouts the year round. There is no need for a garden, as they grow right in the kitchen on the window sill. Sprouts are a favorite with children—they love to watch them grow. It is fun and fascinating.

Sprouts take only a few days from sowing to eating. There is a minimum of mess and bother, and they are not at all expensive, either. They are delicious, crunchy, and healthful.

Buy your seeds at a health food store, if you can. This way you will be sure to get untreated seed.

Items You Might Include:

Mung Bean Seeds	Cheesecloth
Alfalfa Seeds	Small Glass Jars
Cress Seeds	Piece of Flannel
Elastic Bands	Plastic Bags
Book on Sprouting	Recipe Ideas

Homemade Goodies Basket

Summer Treats Basket

There is nothing like a tall, cool, refreshing drink on a hot summer day. Give someone all the fixings, arranged on cool green shredded cellophane; add some fresh-looking white silk daisies for decoration.

Items You Might Include:

Lemons	Oranges
Cherries (in jar)	Soda Water or Perrier
Tall Glasses	Long Stirrers
Iced Drink Spoons	Iced Tea Mix
Lime Cordial Mix	Assorted Syrups

Winter Treats Basket

On a frosty winter day, nothing is better than a delicious, rich, hot drink concoction.

Items You Might Include:

Hot Chocolate Mix	Mugs
Flavored Coffee Mixes	Slippers
Marshmallows	Fluffy Afghan
Latest Bestseller	Cold Remedy

SPECIALTY BASKETS

Specialty baskets are gifts selected for the unique interests of a dear friend, an acquaintance, or a relative: assorted brushes for a favorite uncle, a beauty basket for your best friend, sweet-smelling sachets for the ladies you work with, a shower basket for a new bride, or a basket full of wonderful playthings for a young niece or nephew.

Some of these baskets are decidedly feminine, some masculine, others are suitable for both male and female.

You can make your baskets more personal for *your* friends by including something only *they* would be interested in. Maybe a friend or relative is absolutely addicted to a certain product—bath oil, for example. Consider buying two or three bottles and arranging them in a basket with some silk flowers for decoration. This would make a most welcome gift and you wouldn't have to roam the stores, searching and wondering if the person would like this or that.

Personally, I would much rather receive a bottle of my favorite cologne or a couple of lace handkerchiefs (I have dozens already) than a gift I have no use for.

When someone goes to the bother of finding out exactly what you like, it does mean a great deal. The gift may only cost a few dollars, but it represents more thoughtfulness and love than an expensive present that was bought simply because a present *had* to be bought.

So, before you rush out at the last minute and scoop up that expensive but not necessarily wanted item, stop and think for a moment: you will probably come up with a more appropriate gift at less expense.

Violet or Lavender Basket

Think of violets or lavender and what comes to mind? Sweet little old ladies, I'll bet. But these exquisite, delicate fragrances are far too lovely to be limited to just one age group. Even young children can enjoy them in the form of sachets for dresser drawers.

The following items placed on mauve or purple shredded cellophane look very attractive. Decorate your basket with some silk violets or real lavender if you can get some.

Violet- or Lavender-Scented Items You Might Include:

Soap	Bath Salts*
Talc	Bath Crystals
Cologne	Bath Oil
Perfume	Sachets*
Lavender Water	Lavender Meal
Body Lotion	Bath Cubes

For instructions on how to make the starred items, see Part III of this book.

Women's Soap Basket

There are so many soaps to choose from: they come in all shapes, sizes, and scents, with lots of delightful ingredients.

Mix or match them and create a wonderfully fragrant basket. Wrap the soaps in little circles of fine net fabric (see Part III of this book) and tie with a satin ribbon, in a bow. You could even color code the wrapping to the soap: pink for rose-scented soaps; green for herbal soaps; yellow for lemon or camomile soaps; mauve for lavender or violet soaps; and blue for oatmeal or cold cream soaps.

Soaps You Might Include:

Fruit-Scented	Herbal
Oatmeal	Floral
Cold Cream	Glycerine
Perfumed	Cucumber
Soap-on-a-Rope	Sauna

Manicure Basket

Everyone ought to have a manicure kit—even the very young.

Items You Might Include:

Emery Boards	Nail Buffer
Nail Scissors	Hand Lotion
Cuticle Cream	Nail Polish
Baby Oil	Nail Brush
Orangewood Sticks	Cotton Gloves
Cuticle Remover	Nail Clippers
Cotton Squares	Polish Remover

Lingerie Organizer Basket

Pretty fabric cases help to keep lingerie drawers neat and sweaters clean and tidy. One can see where everything is at a glance, instead of having to rummage through this and that.

The cases are easy to make, yet are so attractive and useful. Everyone can find uses for them. They are made from fabric remnants, so cost is minimal; you can afford to give several to each of your friends or relatives. Place a scented sachet in each case for that little extra touch.

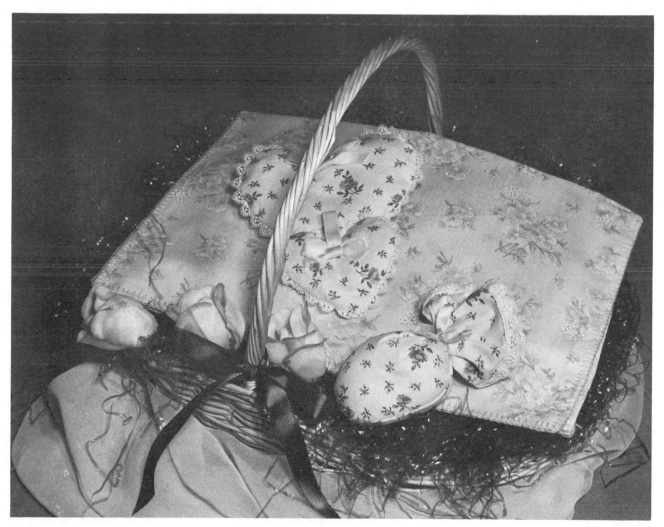

Lingerie Organizer Basket

Part III of this book provides instructions for making lingerie cases, pajama cases, sweater cases, and hosiery cases.

Women's Bath Basket

It is easy to put together a luxury basket any woman would love to receive. If you know the person's favorite scent, then buy the individual items in that fragrance.

Items You Might Include:

Soap	Loofah
Natural Sponge	Bath Oil
Bath Brush	Pumice Stone
Body Lotion	Bath Foam
Shower Cap	Bath Crystals
Bath Salts*	Bath Mat*
Bath Mitt*	Bath Pillow*

Options:
Candles
Herb Bags
Wine

For instructions on how to make the starred items, see Part III of this book.

Women's Bath Basket

Women's Accessories Basket

Mix accessories or match them. Make a belt basket, a scarf basket, or a trinket basket, or fill one basket with different things—scarves, belts, silk flowers, a scarf holder, handkerchiefs.

These baskets look pretty if they are lined with velvet, satin, or fake fur.

Accessories You Might Include:

Scarves	Scarf Holder
Belts	Scarf Pins
Silk Flowers	Gold Chains
Hair Combs	Hair Ornaments
Lapel Pins	Gloves
Fancy Handkerchiefs	

Women's Hosiery Basket

I don't know a woman who wouldn't enjoy receiving one of these baskets. Nylon stockings can be bought in so many colors now, and there are some beautifully textured ones available also.

For a delightful touch of femininity, how about a lovely lacy garter belt with some silk stockings? They have recently been making a comeback and are quite popular.

Items You Might Include:

Nylon Stockings	Tights
Silk Stockings	Anklets
Leg Warmers	Knee Highs
Textured Hose	Sports Socks
Lace Garter Belt	

Sachet Basket

Scented sachets make wonderful little presents that are ideal as gifts for aquaintances you haven't known long, for women you work with, or for those you do not see often but still want to remember on certain occasions.

Sachets are placed in lingerie drawers or closets, on draperies or furniture, under pillows for sweet dreams, or simply left out in tiny containers to scent rooms.

Baskets for sachets can be painted delicate colors and trimmed with bows and flowers.

As an alternative, you could fill small glass containers with the sachet mixture and tie a satin ribbon around the top. Secure the top first with a bit of clear sticky tape. Add a few silk flowers for decoration.

Recipes for sachet mixtures and instructions for sachet bags are given in Part III of this book.

Women's Handkerchief Basket

It is a shame that the lovely lace handkerchief has been replaced by the tissue. Throwaway tissues have their place—as makeup removers or as disposable "hankies" when one has a cold—but a lace-trimmed or finely embroidered handkerchief is so feminine and elegant, especially when scented with a few drops of perfume or when sprinkled with lavender water.

A couple of fancy handkerchiefs, a small bottle

Women's Handkerchief Basket

of lavender water and a few scented sachets are all you need to make a lovely, aromatic gift. They make an excellent "get-well" or "thank-you" gift.

Line your baskets with soft crushed velvet, satin, or plain velvet for a luxurious effect. Decorate with some silk flowers or with real lavender if you can find some.

Men's Bath Basket

If you know the person's favorite scent then purchase the individual ingredients in that fragrance. Add a little humor to the gift by tucking in a small bath toy—such as a boat or a rubber ducky.

Items You Might Include:

Soap	Large Fluffy Towel
Soap-on-a-Rope	Large Fluffy Washcloth
Body Lotion	Toenail Clippers
Pumice Stone	Fingernail Clippers
Loofah	Bath Toy
Bath Mat*	Bath Mitt*
Bath Pillow*	

See Part III of this book for instructions on how to make the starred items.

Men's Grooming Basket

Men's Brush Basket

This is quite a novelty basket, but it's useful and different and makes a marvelous gift for the man who has everything.

You could line the basket with felt or corduroy in an earthy or muted color—hunter green, navy, gold, brown, or maroon.

Brushes You Might Include:

Shoe Brushes	Hairbrushes
Clothes Brushes	Nail Brushes
Bath Brush	Toothbrushes
Shaving Brushes	Complexion Brushes

Men's Grooming Basket

Most companies that used to make just after-shave lotion now manufacture a whole range of products for men. Many different scents are available, including herbal, earthy, leathery, spicy, citrus, and modern blends.

You can purchase everything from shampoo to body lotion, all in the same scent.

Items You Might Include:

Shampoo	Hair Conditioner
Shaving Cream	Shaving Brush
Shaving Soap	Soap Dish
After-Shave Lotion	Cologne
Body Lotion	Talc
Soap	Soap-on-a-Rope
Deodorant	Moisturizers
Combs	Hairbrush

Men's Sock Basket

Choose neutral colors like black, navy, brown, grey, or dark green if you are not familiar with the man's taste in color or pattern.

Roll socks jelly roll–style and stand them upright in a deep basket or lay them side by side in a long, shallow one.

Socks You Might Include:

Regular Socks	Sports Socks
Silk Socks	Work Socks
Cotton Socks	Terrycloth Socks
Corduroy Socks	Extra-long Socks
Suspenders	Hiking Socks

Men's Handkerchief Basket

Men can never have enough handkerchiefs since they use them in so many ways: to shine shoes, to polish cars, to clean oil dip sticks, to clean windows, to clean fountain pens, as paint rags, and as all-around dusters.

Pure cotton handkerchiefs are the best; however, you may have to settle for polyester or at least a blend of fibers.

There is no need to stick to plain white—handkerchiefs now come in a variety of nice colors and patterns. You may also come across monogrammed handkerchiefs, although probably only in the larger stores.

Roll each handkerchief and stand it up in a small deep basket, or lay the handkerchiefs side by side in a shallow one.

Men's Handkerchief Basket

Men's Sock Basket

You might also combine handkerchiefs with socks—a good gift idea for college students away from home.

Book Basket

This is a basket that will appeal to all bookworms. Fill a small basket with books that the recipient would like to read.

Books You Might Include:

Science Fiction	Gardening
Historical	Cooking
Romance	Hobby
Western	Natural Science
Adventure	Best-Sellers
Mysteries	Your Own Favorite Titles

Options:
Unusual Bookmarks
Bookplates
Magazine Subscription(s)

Stationery Basket

We all write letters at some time or another; having everything together right at hand is a great help. It is also extra nice to write our thoughts on decorative notepaper with envelopes to match, but how many of us actually buy these items for ourselves? We usually just grab a pad of ordinary white paper.

This gift will be more appreciated than you think.

Items You Might Include:

Notepaper   Pen and Holder
Thank-You Notes   Stamps
Envelopes   Address Book
Fancy Notes

Options:
Calligraphy Pen Set
Book on Calligraphy
Ink

Picnic Items Basket

Beach Basket

Everyone needs protection from the sun and its harmful, drying effects. Men, women, and children alike are vulnerable when it comes to being out in the heat.

Baskets should have handles for easy carrying. Terrycloth makes an ideal lining fabric for beach baskets.

Items You Might Include:

Suntan Lotion	Hat
After-Sun Lotion	Sun Visor
Lip Balm	Beach Pillow*
Medicated Cream	Large Fluffy Towel
Sunburn Ointment	Inflatable Beach Ball
Terrycloth Cover-up	

For directions on how to make the beach pillow, see Part III of this book.

Picnic Items Basket

Imagine the pleasure of receiving a well-stocked picnic basket, all ready to go at a moment's notice! Purchase an authentic picnic basket or simply use a large, deep basket with handles.

The basket may be lined with the same fabric used for the tablecloth and napkins.

Items You Might Include:

Tablecloth*	Forks, Knives,
Napkins*	Spoons
Napkin Holders*	Plates
Cutlery Holders*	Cups
Can Opener	Small Bowls
Small Condiment	Salt and Pepper
Containers	Mills

See Part III of this book for instructions on how to make starred items.

"Get-Well" Basket

There is nothing more boring than lying in bed, waiting to get better after a bout of illness or an operation. Anything that relieves the monotony is most welcome.

Choose a small basket, since hospital space is usually very limited. Don't bother with packing material or a lot of trimming. Just present a simple basket filled with the chosen items plus a card full of warm get-well wishes.

Items You Might Include:

Notepaper, Pens	Stamps
Crossword Puzzle Book	Envelopes
Pocket Dictionary	Miniature
Small Needlework Projects	Games
Imported Biscuits	Books
Playing Cards	Magazines
Soap, Talc, and Cologne	Fruit
with a Light, Fresh Scent	

"Get-Well" Basket

Bartender's Basket

A bartender's basket is an ideal basket for someone who has just added a bar to his or her home. Actually, it also makes a nice gift for someone who doesn't have a bar, since the basket itself acts as a portable "bar" with all the equipment inside it.

Items You Might Include:

Cocktail Shaker	Fancy Toothpicks
Ice Bucket	Jar of Olives
Long Stirrers	Ice Tongs
Jar of Cherries	Bottle Opener
Corkscrew	Ice Cube Tray
Stir Sticks	Bar Jiggers
Coasters	Ice Bag
Book on How to Mix Drinks	Bitters

Car Care Basket

Cars have to be taken care of, just as people do. They have to be cleaned, washed, and polished, not just so that they will look nice but to protect them from the elements.

Going through a car wash isn't the same as washing the car yourself. You can do a much better job, and with a kit like the one below you can do a super job.

Items You Might Include:

Wash Cloths	Window Cleaner
Sponges	Tire Cleaner
Upholstery Cleaner	Soap
Chrome Polish	Miniature Vacuum
Car Wax	Soft Brush
Wash Mitt*	Polishing Mitt*
Vinyl Cleaner	Car Deodorizer

See Part III of this book for details on how to make starred items.

Pet Care Basket

Any cat or dog would love to have such a basket for his or her birthday or as Christmas present. Each basket should include a comfy cushion, some playthings, and a few treats.

There are baskets available that are made especially for pets; they are available in graded sizes from very small to gigantic. If you can't find these at your local stores, you could use a regular basket in a suitable size.

Items You Might Include:

Pet Cushion*	Pet Toys*
Collar and Leash	Food Dishes
Food	Dog Biscuits
Rawhide Pieces	Chew Bones
Chew Sticks	Fresh Catnip
Favorite Nibbles	Scratch Boards
Pet Care Book	Dog Shampoo
Water Dish	Pet Treats
Pet Blanket	Dog Booties
Nail Clippers	Brush

Instructions for making starred items are in Part III of this book.

Pet Care Basket

BASKETS FOR BABIES AND CHILDREN

Children are so easy to please—they like everything. Give them a basket filled to overflowing with assorted playthings, and they will be positively ecstatic.

You can forget all about the packing material and trimmings (except in certain baskets for little girls). Children are not interested in all that "stuff"; all they want are the toys and other goodies in the basket.

However, this does not mean that the basket shouldn't be wrapped. Children do like surprises, and they love to unwrap things and discover what is inside. You might consider wrapping each item separately for lots of little surprises and then piling them all in a basket for a grab bag effect.

There are novelty baskets available, but these can be quite expensive. You may prefer to use a regular-shaped basket unless you come across a bargain somewhere.

Baby baskets can be painted in pastel colors—pale yellow, pink, blue, mint green, or peach—or in pure white.

Decorate baby baskets with tiny bows, and line them with pretty fabric. Satin or velvet in the same color as the basket looks especially delightful.

Babies' Toy Basket

You could fill this basket with age-graded toys: a few infant toys, such as mobiles or rattles; one or two soft cuddly toys for later; and a learning toy or two for later still. Fill the whole basket with a particular type of toy if you want a gift that is specialized.

Toys You Might Include:

Soft Cuddly Toys	Soft Balls
Rattles	Teething Toys
Mobiles	Musical Toys
Learning Toys	Music Box

Layette Basket

Babies are completely re-dressed at least four or five times a day, so mothers need a good supply of clothing (not to mention patience). They can never have too many different sizes of infant wear, since what fits baby today probably won't fit him or her next week. Keep this in mind when shopping and buy a few assorted sizes rather than a lot of one size.

Items You Might Include:

Tiny Vests	Hats
Nightgowns	Mittens
Matinée Jackets	Booties
Sleepers	Bibs
Plastic Pants	Shawl
Box of Pure Soap Flakes	

Diaper Basket

If there is anything a mother needs more of than clothing for her little darling, it is diapers—mountains of them.

Items You Might Include:

Diapers	Vaseline
Diaper Pins	Wet Towels
Diaper Rash Cream	Baby Powder
Plastic Pants	Changing Pads

Babies' Blanket Basket

These items usually get changed frequently too, so it helps to have a good supply, especially crib sheets. Receiving blankets seem to get more than their fair share of use also.

Items You Might Include:

Fluffy Blanket	Baby Afghan
Receiving Blankets	Baby Quilt
Crib Sheets	Shawl
Box of Pure Soap Flakes	

Babies' Bath Basket

Everyone has to bathe, and baby is no exception—he or she simply needs special products.

Items You Might Include:

Bath Lotion	Baby Oil
Baby Lotion	Cotton Swabs
Baby Soap	Soft Towels
Baby Powder	Soft Washcloths
Baby Shampoo	Bath Support
Cotton Balls	Bath Toy

Babies' Feeding Basket

This basket should include lots of bibs and washcloths, since food has a tendency to go everywhere except the baby's mouth and since, once it does get in, there is no guarantee it will stay there.

Items You Might Include:

Bibs	Baby Washcloths
Baby Food Dish	Baby Towel
Feeding Spoons	Baby Cup
Large Apron for Mother	

Babies' Bath Basket

Children's Bath Basket

Use the big, fluffy towel as a soft bed for the items you choose.

Items You Might Include:

Large, Fluffy Towel	Soap
Washcloth	Sponge
Children's Shampoo	Nail Clippers
Bath Mitt*	Bath Mat*
Bath Toys	Body Lotion
Bath Foam	

See Part III of this book for details on how to make starred items.

Little Beauty Basket

Little girls enjoy being pampered just like their big sisters. With this gift they will feel very special. Buy baby products in their standard containers and transfer them to pretty bottles, attaching fancy labels.

Items You Might Include:

Creme Rinse	Talcum Powder
Children's Cologne	Body Lotion
Children's Lip Balm	Soap
Shampoo	

Pretty Hair Basket

Give this basket to a little girl, and watch her eyes light up. She will want to wash and "style" her hair every fifteen minutes.

Fold the hair ribbons and secure them with a colored barrette in the middle to keep them in order.

Items You Might Include:

Children's Shampoo	Barrettes
Children's Creme Rinse	Fancy Bobby Pins
Brush	Comb
Hair Ribbons	Coated Elastics

Children's Soap Basket

Stuff the basket with many different kinds of soap, each wrapped in its own little wrapper.

Items You Might Include:

Animal-shaped Soap	Sponge
Fruit-shaped Soap	Baby Soap
Cartoon Character– shaped Soaps	

Children's Beach Basket

Choose a basket with handles: the smallest one that will hold the items you select.

Items You Might Include:

Suntan Lotion	Towel
After-Sun Lotion	Sun Hat
Beach Shoes	Beach Toys
Water Wings	Swimsuit
Sunglasses	Small Pail
Spade	Beach Ball

Little Beauty Basket

Games Basket

What child doesn't like to play games? With this basket, the child and his or her friends can have a marvelous time.

Items You Might Include:

Jumprope	Tiddlywinks
Pick-up Sticks	Puzzles
Baseball Mitt	Bat
Jacks	Marbles
Children's Playing Cards	Crayons and Book
Anything Else You Can Find!	

School Basket

Starting school can be quite traumatic. Make it a bit more enjoyable with a special school basket chock-full of useful things.

School Items You Might Include:

Pens and Pencils	Notebooks
Pencil Case	Paper
Schoolbag	Pencil Set
Lunchbox	Dictionary

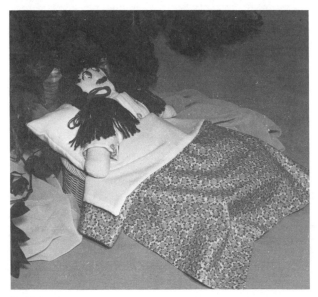

Doll Basket

Arts and Crafts Basket

If the child is interested in one particular hobby, fill the basket with items related to that hobby; or, start the child on a new pastime.

Wander through your local craft store, and you will come up with a lot more ideas than I have included here.

Items You Might Include:

Modeling Clay	Construction Paper
Coloring Books	Colored Pencils
Crayons	Watercolor Paints
White Glue	Blunt-Tipped Scissors
Felt Pieces	
Fake Fur Pieces	Pasta Shapes
Chenille Stems	Paper Shapes
Beads (older kids only)	Craft Sticks
	Apron or Smock
Beading Thread	Plastic Sheet
Small Hobby Kits	Molded Foam Forms
Craft Books	

Doll Basket

Any rectangular or oval shape would do for this basket, but some stores carry a basket shaped like a miniature baby cradle. In Part III of this book, you will find instructions for making all of the following items.

Items You Might Include:

Mattress	Sheets
Pillow	Pillowcase
Blanket	Bedspread
Little Cloth Doll with Nightgown	

Little Bookworm's Basket

Find out if the child is interested in anything special (stamps, animals, or ships, for example), then buy books on that subject. Include a few children's bookmarks and maybe a subscription to a favorite magazine.

Books You Might Include:

Children's Stories
Classics
Activity Books
Educational Books
Informational Books

Comic Books
Coloring Books
Picture Books
Hobby Books
Notebooks

Sprout Basket

See the Sprout Basket described in the Gourmet Baskets section.

Shoeshine Basket

This should be the child's very own shoeshine kit. The child who receives this basket probably will not have to be told to keep his or her shoes clean: the novelty of having his or her own polishes, cloths, and so on will be enough motivation. A nice little kit can be made up if you find a small basket with a lid.

Items You Might Include:

Assorted Shoe Polishes
Polishing Cloths
Spare Shoelaces

Plastic Sheet
Shoe Brushes

Easter Basket

Fill a basket with colored, shredded cellophane, and then tuck a few chocolate eggs and bunnies into it. Include some small toys and maybe a book or two in the basket instead of a lot of sugary candy.

Junior Outdoor Gardener's Basket

A deep, square basket works well here: one with handles on both sides. For seeds, select anything that a child likes to eat and that is easy to grow from seeds, such as radishes, beans, carrots, and beets.

Items You Might Include:

Small Garden Tools
Gardening Gloves
Children's Book about
    Gardening
Wooden Popsicle Sticks
    (for markers)

Sun Hat
Ball of String
Small Wooden
    Stakes
Watering Can
Seeds

Junior Indoor Gardener's Basket

If there is no outdoor garden space available, this is the next best thing.

Items You Might Include:

Medium-Sized Flat
    Container
Tiny Indoor Garden
    Tools
Plastic Sprayer
Children's Book about
    House Plants

Soil
Charcoal
Tiny Plants
Cress Seeds
Watering Can
Small Bag of
    Gravel

Junior Indoor Gardener's Basket

BASKETS FOR BRIDES

The basket ideas that follow are primarily for bridal showers; however, they do make marvelous housewarming gifts also.

Some of the gifts may seem a bit mundane, but remember that when one is just starting out one needs everything. At the risk of repeating myself, it is much better to receive something you really need than some exotic but ridiculous item you will never have any use for.

If, for example, you have been using certain cleaning products for some time and have had good results with them, by all means fill a basket with the same brands and give it to a new bride at her shower. This makes more sense than giving maybe a spice rack or tea kettle, of which she will probably get two or three anyway.

So, put your imagination to work again and you'll come up with a lot more ideas than I have given here.

Kitchen Basket

A kitchen basket can be color-coordinated to the recipient's kitchen if you know her color scheme.

Items You Might Include:

Oven Mitts	Aprons
Pot Holders	Dish Towels
Tea Towels	Trivets

Dining Table Basket

Color-coordinate the items in this basket to the recipient's dining room or kitchen. See Part III of this book for details on how to make the starred items.

Items You Might Include:

Tablecloth*	Placemats*
Napkins*	Coasters
Napkin Holders*	Tea Cozy*
Egg Cozies*	

Bed Linens Basket

A bed set usually consists of a top sheet, a bottom sheet, and two pillowcases.

Alternatively, you could give just pillowcases, in plain colors—white, green, yellow, beige. Buy them on sale and take advantage of the savings.

With sheets and blankets, it might be best to buy at regular prices so they can be returned if the size is wrong.

Items You Might Include:

Plain Sheets	Pillowcases
Patterned Sheets	Satin Sheets
Flannel Sheets	Blankets
Pillows	Mattress Cover

Towel Basket

Roll the towels up, jelly roll–style, and lay them side by side in a shallow basket or stand them up in a deep one.

A towel set includes one bath towel, one hand towel, and one facecloth. These could be folded and placed on top of each other.

Towels You Might Include:

Bath Towels	Hand Towels
Extra-Large Towels	Guest Towels
Facecloths	Beach Towels
Monogrammed Towels	

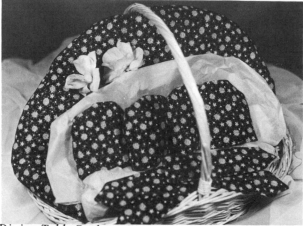

Dining Table Basket

Utensil Basket

Place utensils in a long bread-type basket, or stand them upright in a deep one.

Utensils You Might Include:

Wooden Spoons	Wooden Stirrers
Rolling Pin	Wooden Mallet
Spatulas	Spaghetti Stirrer
Soup Ladle	Egg Lifter
Vegetable Servers	Tongs
Meat Thermometer	Cheese Grater
Wire Whisks	Pastry Brush
Vegetable Peeler	Meat Baster
Vegetable Slicer	Cake Server
Candy Thermometer	Icing Gun
Bottle Opener	Jar Opener
Kitchen Scissors	Potato Masher
Pastry Cutter	Cheese Cutter

Small Utensil Basket

These are little items people never remember to buy for themselves.

Walk through the housewares department of any large store and you will find dozens of handy little gadgets like those listed here. Kitchen boutiques are good places to browse also.

Utensils You Might Include:

Garlic Press	Cookie Cutters
Donut Cutter	Cheese Cutter
Lemon Zester	Meat Skewers
Apple Corer	Can Opener
Fruit Pitter	Bottle Caps
Grapefruit Knife	Miniature Grater
Vegetable Slicer	Coffee Measure
Orange Peeler	Nutmeg Grater

Baking Pan Basket

The size of the basket you need will depend on the type of pans you choose, so pick the pans first. Each style of pan usually comes in different sizes, so you can fill a basket exclusively with pie pans or cake pans, for example.

Items You Might Include:

Pie Pans	Muffin Pans
Bundt Pans	Flan Dishes
Round Cake Pans	Square Cake Pans
Springform Pans	Angelfood Cake Pan
Bread Pans	Cookie Sheets
Souffle Dishes	Clay Baker
Pizza Pans	Casserole Dishes
Cookbooks	

Ramekin Basket

Ramekins are dishes used for serving soups, beans, small casseroles, chicken pies, and other such foods.

Some ramekins have handles on both sides, some have a handle on one side only, and some have no handles at all. Some have lids, while others do not. No matter what form they take, they are very useful items to have in the kitchen.

Tuck the ramekins in shredded cellophane, parchment excelsior, or tissue paper. Include a cookbook if you wish.

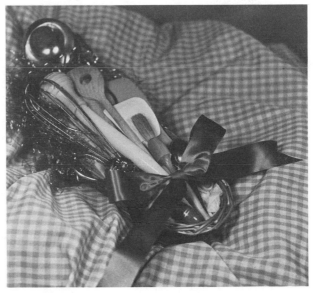

Utensil Basket

Measuring Set Basket

Measuring spoons and cups are available in glass, stainless steel, and plastic. Take your pick: they are all good, although plastic may not be dishwasher-safe.

Items You Might Include:

Measuring Spoons	Measuring Cups
Kitchen Scales	Coffee Measure

Cups and Saucers Basket

Fancy cups and saucers make a lovely gift, and this type of china does not have to match.

There are many beautiful designs and patterns from which to choose, ranging in price from quite cheap to very expensive. The size of the basket you need will depend on how many sets you wish to give. Fill the basket with shredded cellophane or parchment excelsior; then stand the saucers

Measuring Set Basket

Cups and Saucers Basket

up at the back of the basket, and tuck them down slightly in the bedding. Stand the cups at an angle in front of the saucers.

Mug Basket

Mugs are very handy for everyday use. You will find quite a variety in any gift or department store.

Give two or more, nestled in shredded cellophane or tissue paper.

If you can find mugs with removable lids, buy them. They really work and make lovely novelty gifts.

Juice Basket

Juice sets come in all sizes, shapes, and materials. They usually consist of from four to eight small glasses and a juice container. However, the package sometimes leaves much to be desired. Simply transfer the set to a suitably sized basket, filled with cellophane or excelsior.

If you can't find a set that catches your eye, buy the glasses and container separately. Include a long stirrer and maybe a book on how to make and mix juices.

Knife Basket

A long, bread-type basket filled with crumpled tissue works well, as does a shallow, rectangular one. Knives may be wrapped in tissue paper before being placed in the basket.

Knives You Might Include:

Paring Knife	Cake Knife
Meat Cleaver	Carving Knife
French Knife	Fruit Knives
Steak Knives	Electric Knife

Options:
Cutting Board
Knife Sharpener

Juice Basket

Candle Basket

Place a couple of tall candles and a pair of attractive candle sticks on top of shredded cellophane in a long narrow basket.

Scented candles are also lovely as gifts and often come in glass containers. Look for the newer sculptured candles too. Votive candles are quite popular now and can be found in most large stores.

A candle boutique, if there is one near you, is a perfect place to shop. They carry candles you wouldn't see anywhere else.

Include a candle snuffer and a box of extra long matches.

Cookbook Basket

A set of two, three, or four cookbooks in a basket tied with a ribbon makes a useful and attractive gift. There is a wide variety of books—general and specialized—available, so you will have no trouble filling this basket.

Choose from international cuisines, entrées, salads, meats, desserts, beverages, books on nutrition, books on preserving foods, and many other possibilities.

Paperbacks make ideal choices; they are not expensive, and they are all the same size.

Clean-up Basket

Clean-up Basket

Use a large basket, and fill it with assorted items; or fill a smaller basket with specialty cleaners—such as for the bathroom or kitchen.

Items You Might Include:

Dish Detergent	Floor Cleaner
Powder Cleanser	Disinfectant
Soap Pads	Bathroom Cleanser
Scouring Pads	Room Deodorizer
Teflon Cleaner	Furniture Polish
Silver Cleaner	Counter Cleaner
Wire Cleaning Pads	Scrub Brush
Rubber Gloves	Cleaning Cloths
Sponges	Polishing Cloths
Floor Wax	Window Cleaner
Chrome Polish	Lemon Oil

Laundry Basket

Use a clothes basket or hamper and place your favorite laundry products inside. If this type of basket is a little out of the reach of your pocketbook, pack a regular deep basket that has handles.

Items You Might Include:

Laundry Detergent	Cold Water Wash
Bleach	Prewash Soak
Fabric Softener	Pure Soap Flakes

Dishwasher's Basket

Not everyone owns an automatic dishwasher, so in some cases this basket would be most appreciated.

Items You Might Include:

Dish Detergent	Dish Mop
Bottle Brushes	Teflon Cleaner
Soap Pads	Steel Wool Pads
Dishcloths	Dish Towels
Sponges	Soap Pad Dish
Aprons	Hand Cream

HOBBY BASKETS

There are as many hobbies as there are people, and most people have at least one—collecting, painting, reading, gardening, sewing, or maybe some sport.

It would be impossible to list all hobbies here; however, I have given suggestions for a few baskets to get the idea across.

To make up hobby baskets for your friends, find out what their interests are and fill the baskets with items related to these interests. It might be a good idea to read about the hobby first, so you know what to purchase and what not to. Also, determine if your friend is a beginner at the hobby or more advanced. Some hobbies can be pursued at various levels, and you should keep this in mind.

Books on hobbies are very popular—bookstores are full of them. Again, the level of your friend's interest in the hobby should be considered: don't buy a book on advanced techniques for a beginner, or vice versa.

Of course, you could always introduce someone to a brand new hobby.

Indoor Gardener's Basket

Make a specialized garden basket—african violets, succulents, cacti, carnivorous plants, or some other plant family. You can buy ready-mixed potting soil, or you can make up your own.

Items You Might Include:

Small Plants	Plant Food
Potting Soil	Miniature Tools
Charcoal	Spray Bottle
Sand	Waterproof
Vermiculite	Container
Pebbles or Gravel	Plastic Sheets
Watering Can	Small Stakes
Book about Houseplants	

Outdoor Gardener's Basket

For a specialized basket, include only flower seeds, vegetable seeds, or herb seeds, plus a book on how to grow them.

Items You Might Include:

Small Garden Tools	Various Seeds
Gardening Gloves	Plant Food
Sun Hat	Marker Sticks
Garden Garbage Bags	Kneeling Pad
Knee Pads	Wooden Stakes
Book on Organic	Book on Basic
Gardening	Gardening

Flower Arranger's Basket

This is a delightful hobby, and, with silk flowers becoming more popular and realistic-looking, one does not have to rely on expensive fresh flowers to indulge in it.

Items You Might Include:

Foam Blocks	Wire Cutters
Small Knife	Spray Bottle
Florist's Wire	Anchoring Clay
Pin Holders	Anchoring Tape
Colored Pebbles	Wooden Picks
Small Containers	Orchid Tubes
Candle Cup Holder	Band-Aids
Book about Flower	
Arranging	

Candle Maker's Basket

Many people enjoy making their own candles. It is a fascinating hobby, and supplies can be obtained quite easily at craft shops.

Items You Might Include:

Paraffin Wax	Candle Molds
Beeswax	Mold Release
Stearic Acid	Mold Cleaner
Luster Crystals	Ice Pick
Wicking	Candle Color
Wick Holders	Candle Scent
Candy Thermometer	Mold Sealer

Knitter's Basket

A large basket—a deep bucket-type—can be used here, and it can be lined with pretty cotton fabric. It can afterward be used as a knitting storage basket.

Items You Might Include:

Knitting Needle Case	Stitch Holders
Knitting Needles	Needle Sizer
Row Counters	Notebook and Pen
Cable Needles	Cloth Tape Measure
Row Markers	Bodkins

Sewer's Basket

Use a fairly deep basket with a lid, if you can find one. Line it with felt, using Method #2 for Square or Rectangular Linings (see page 19).

Individual items can be placed in small boxes so they don't become all mixed together.

Knitter's Basket

Items You Might Include:

Sewing Needles	Scissors
Straight Pins	Seam Ripper
Cloth Tape Measure	Thimbles
Pin Cushion	Thread
Needle Threader	Thread Wax
Marking Chalk	Hooks and Eyes
Dressmaker's Carbon	Tracing Wheel
Press Studs	Darning Thread

Fisherman's Basket

See if you can find a wicker fishing creel. If you cannot locate one of these, use a fairly deep basket with a lid.

Items You Might Include:

Fishhooks	Fish Scaler
Flies	Fish Knife
Lures	Fishing Line
Floats	First Aid Kit
Sinker Weights	Insect Repellent
Fish Weighing Scales	Hat

Sportsman's Basket

Fill a basket with items suitable for your sportsminded friends—be they golfers, tennis players, ball players, sailing buffs, or whatever. Include a few items that are more generally useful.

Items You Might Include:

First Aid Products	Suntan Lotion
Insect Repellent	Small Towels
Talcum Powder	Facecloth
Medicated Cream	Sweat Bands
Sun Hat or Visor	Small Thermos
Lip Balm	Wet Towels

Beader's Basket

Craft stores usually carry a wonderful variety of beads in a wide range of materials. One can make all kinds of lovely things, from necklaces and bracelets to key chains and ornaments.

Older children enjoy this craft, too. However, it is not for the very young (children under five).

Items You Might Include:

Plastic Beads	Glass Beads
Rocaille Beads	Seed Beads
Pony Beads	Bugle Beads
Flower Beads	Mosaic Beads
Propeller Beads	Dazzle Beads
Beading Thread	Pearls
Jewelry Findings	Tubular Beads
Gold and Silver Beads	Limoges Beads
Beading Needles	Sequins
Beading Elastic	Sundiscs
Belt Buckles	Wooden Beads
Beading Loom	Novelty Beads
Books about Beading	Small Kits

Shell Collector's Basket

Some people (I am one of them) love seashells. There are so many different kinds—from large and beautiful pink conchs to tiny but intricate periwinkles.

Some of the more common shells can be bought in bulk at very reasonable prices. They can be used to decorate boxes, mirrors, and wall plaques. Others can be used to make collages or jewelry.

Items You Might Include:

Assorted Sea Shells	White Glue
Gold Paint	Brushes
Small Wooden Boxes	Clear Glaze
Small Wooden Plaques	Jewelry Findings
Book about Seashell Craft	

Calligraphy Basket

Calligraphy is the art of beautiful writing. One does not have to take a course in calligraphy or have a degree in penmanship to be able to enjoy this art form.

Actually the pen does all the work; all one has to do is guide it. A little practice, and one can write in a number of different styles.

Items You Might Include:

Calligraphy Set or Calligraphy Pen and Nibs	Parchment Paper and Envelopes
Ink	Book about Calligraphy

Macramé Basket

By mastering a few basic knots, one can make many lovely items, such as plant hangers, belts, towel holders, lamp shades, and wall hangings.

Items You Might Include:

Macramé Cord	Jute
Macramé Leathers	Waxed Thread
Metal Rings	Macramé Beads
Wooden Rings	Macramé Rods
Belt Buckles	T-Pins
Macramé Board	Purse Handles
Macramé Instruction Book	Small Macramé Kits

Découpage Basket

Just about anything can be découpaged—boxes, bottles, cans, wall plaques. It is easy and fun to do. Supplies are as close as your local craft shop.

Items You Might Include:

Small Wooden Plaques	Wooden Boxes
Wooden Key Tags	White Glue
Découpage Sealer	Découpage Finish
Découpage Thinner	Finishing Wax
Steel Wool (No. 0000)	Wet or Dry Sandpaper
Sanding Block	Brushes
Découpage Scissors	Tweezers
Découpage Decals	Book about Découpage

Batik Basket

Batik is an age-old craft that consists of applying liquid wax to cloth, letting it dry, and then dying the fabric. This process is repeated until a pattern or design is completed. The wax is then removed to leave only the design on the fabric.

Many lovely items can made using batik, including pillows, lamp shades, clothes, wall hangings, and toys.

Items You Might Include:

Unbleached Cotton Fabric	Batik Wax
Alcohol Lamp	Batik Brushes
Batik Stretcher Frame	Tjanting Needle
Book about Batik	Fabric Dyes

Resin Casting Basket

Paperweights, ashtrays, and bookends are a few of the items that can be make with resin. It is a simple yet rewarding hobby.

Items You Might Include:

Clear Casting Resin	Catalyst
Opaque Dye	Resin Cleaner
Transparent Dye	Plastic Polish
Mixing Cups	Wooden Stir
Eyedropper	Sticks
Molds	Fine Sandpaper
Plastic Sheets	Mold Release
Book about Resin Casting	Embedments

GOODWILL BASKETS

Although these "baskets" can be given all year round, Thanksgiving and Christmas seem to be the most popular times for giving them. They are simply sturdy cardboard boxes covered with fabric or paper. Items are piled in or put into little bags first. Bags are tied with ribbon bows.

You could make one large "basket" or several small ones, then take them over to the nearest hospital or Salvation Army office (or to any other organization that helps needy people).

You can start filling goodwill baskets in January. Every time you have a spare piece of fabric or wool, make a soft toy, a hat, or pair of baby booties. Soon you will have quite a collection of items, and you won't even have missed the few dollars they cost.

Think of how many people you could help this way and of the joy and satisfaction you will get from doing it. Persuade your friends and relatives to start baskets of their own, or to contribute to your baskets.

Soft Toy Basket

Make the toys yourself from scraps of fabric. Look for toy patterns at fabric stores or design the toys yourself. You could even use the pattern in Part III of this book and make up a dozen or so little cloth dolls. Odds and ends of wool can also be knitted or crocheted into small toys.

Accessories Basket

Warm scarves, mittens, hats, socks, and baby items can all be made from leftover yarns. These items don't take long to make and are small enought to carry with you, to be worked on in spare moments.

Produce Basket

If you have a garden, you undoubtedly have excess fruits and vegetables. Pack some small "baskets" and take them to your church. Churches are more than glad to distribute food parcels to needy families.

Part Three

Making Items for Baskets

Custom-made items are far superior to store-bought ones, and are less expensive, too. When we make something ourselves, we can take the time necessary to produce an item of quality and durability. Also, we are not limited to the store's choice of colors, patterns or sizes. We have a much wider selection from which we can obtain the exact materials needed for our project.

As an example, I saw a toy mouse in a pet store; it cost $3.98. It consisted of a piece of cotton, with frayed edges, stuffed to resemble (only nearly) the shape of a mouse. This shape was glued (not very well) to a cardboard base. A few loose black threads were the whiskers. In contrast, the little mouse in this book is securely sewn out of felt, with no loose threads to catch in a cat's throat or lodge in its intestines. It even has the allure of fresh catnip, and—what's more—it looks like a mouse. It costs less than 70¢ to make.

All the projects in this book are easy to make. You need no special knowledge or expertise—just the desire to make someone happy.

Cheesecloth Bags
(for Bouquet Garni and Fines Herbes Baskets)

These little bags can be cut from cheesecloth or from fine white net (tulle). Cut 6" × 6" squares or circles with 6" diameters.

Place your herbal mixture in the center of the fabric piece (use several thicknesses for each bag if you are using cheesecloth). Gather the fabric up around the herbs and secure it with white thread or plain dental floss. Use about two feet of thread; after knotting around the center of bag, knot the loose ends together. The thread "handle" then hangs outside the pan and aids in removing the herbs before serving the food. See Figure III-1.

Bath Salts
(for Violet and Lavender and Women's Bath Baskets)

A handful of these fragrant salts in a tub of warm water will gently relax one and erase the day's tensions.

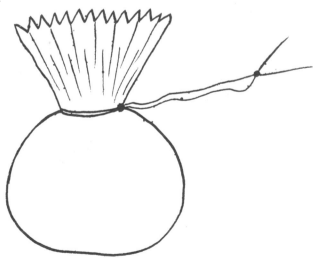

Figure III–1. Cheesecloth Bag.

They are so easy and inexpensive to make that it seems ridiculous to pay triple the cost (or more) for store-bought varieties.

You can use any cologne or perfume as the scent for the bath salts. Lavender, violet, carnation, and lemon are especially nice.

When adding the color, be stingy (color cannot be removed, so add it a drop at a time until you get the required tint); pastel tints look the prettiest, and it only takes a drop or two of color to produce a lovely pale hue.

Make the bath salts ahead of time so they can age for a week or two. Store them in a cool, dark place.

Ingredients:
2 cups Epsom Salts
2 cups Coarse Salt
A few drops Food Coloring
A few drops Scent
Pretty Glass Jars

Measure the salts into a large bowl, and mix them together thoroughly. Add food coloring, one drop at a time, until the salts have picked it up. Add the scent the same way. Fill the containers with the mixture and secure the tops with one or two pieces of cellophane tape. This recipe makes enough salts to fill from two to four containers, depending on the size of the jars.

Decorate each jar with a ribbon bow and silk flowers. Attach an identification label. If you wish, you can decorate the inside of the jar, too. To do this, simply use white glue to attach tiny pressed flowers or découpage decals to the inside of the jar. Make sure the right side of the decoration is to the glass. The glue will dry clear, and you will have a lovely container for your bath salts.

Sachets
(for Sachet Baskets)

Sachets are little bags filled with an aromatic mixture of herbs and spices.

They are tucked into lingerie drawers, pinned behind drapery or furniture, hung in closets, put under pillows, or simply piled into a little basket or container and left on a table or shelf to scent a room.

Pouches can be made from any lightweight fabric, such as cotton, organdy, silk, lawn, batiste, satin, gingham, or tulle (gathered pouch only).

Being so small, they can be made from the tiniest scrap of fabric; don't throw away any leftover material, no matter how small the pieces. Do use only lightweight fabrics, though, so the scent can permeate easily.

Some very pretty pouches can be made by covering plain fabric with an overlay of fine lace. To do this, simply cut identical pieces from fabric and lace. Baste the lace pieces to the corresponding fabric pieces, with the wrong side of the lace to the right side of the fabric. Baste $\frac{1}{2}''$ in from the edges. Then use each piece as you would a single piece of fabric when constructing the pouch.

Choose the shape you want your pouches to be and make a paper pattern. See Figures III-3, III-4, and III-5.

Lay the paper pattern on your fabric piece and cut out the fabric with scissors or pinking shears.

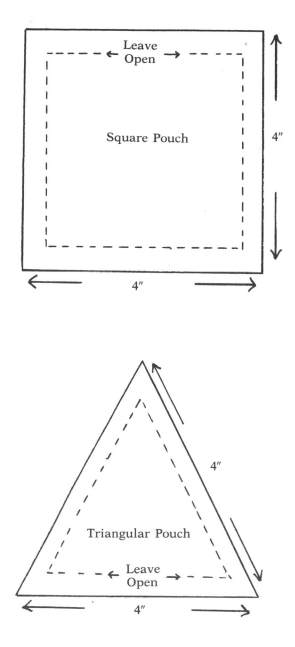

Figure III-3. Pattern for square and triangular pouches for sachets.

Figure III-2. Sachets.

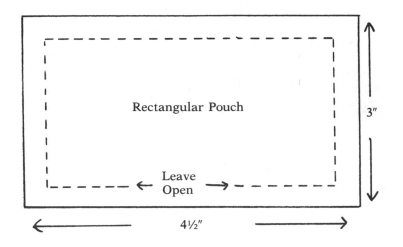

Rectangular Pouch

3"

Leave
Open

4½"

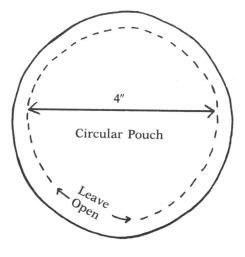

4"

Circular Pouch

Leave
Open

Figure III–4. Patterns for rectangular and circular pouches for sachets.

Basic Pouch

Place the fabric pieces right sides together, and pin. Stitch, using regular machine stitch, $\frac{1}{2}''$ in from the edges all around the pouch, leaving a small $\frac{1}{2}''$ opening along one side. Trim off the corners just above the stitching line. Turn the pouch right side out, and push out the corners with the tips of your scissors.

Fill the pouch with one of the sachet mixtures described below, then blind stitch (refer to Figure I-6) across the opening.

Gathered Pouch

Cut out circles of fabric with 6″ diameters, using pinking shears. Place 1–2 tbsp of one of the sachet mixtures in the center of each circle. Gather up the fabric around the herbs and secure with a small elastic band. Tie a satin ribbon around the band and finish with a bow. Add a tiny silk flower.

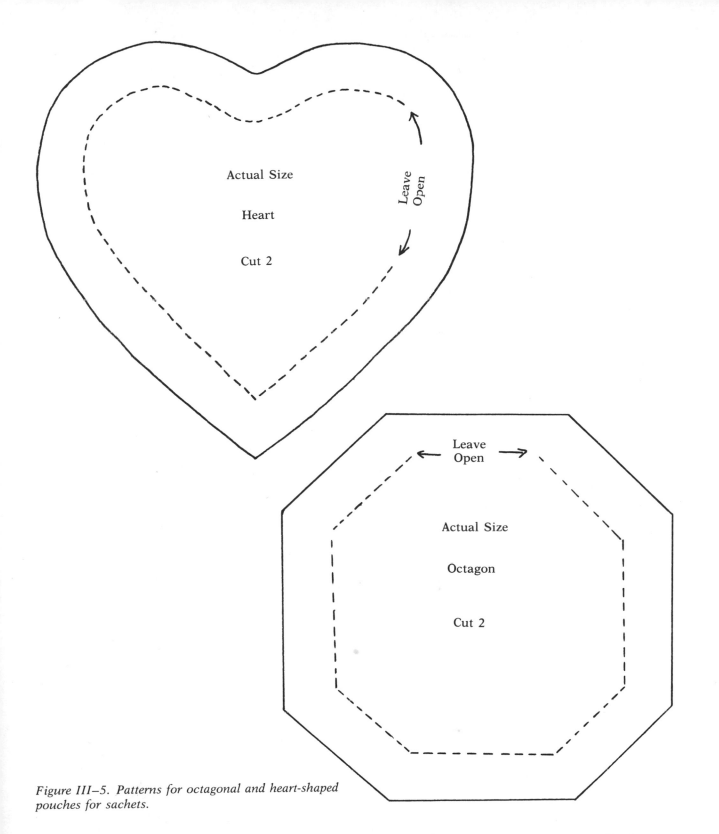

Actual Size

Heart

Cut 2

Leave Open

Leave Open

Actual Size

Octagon

Cut 2

Figure III–5. Patterns for octagonal and heart-shaped pouches for sachets.

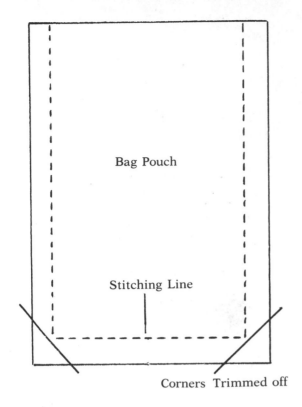

Bag Pouch

Stitching Line

Corners Trimmed off

Figure III–6. Bag pouch for a sachet.

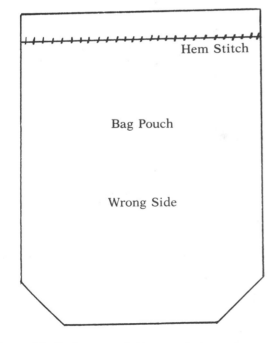

Hem Stitch

Bag Pouch

Wrong Side

Figure III–7. Bag pouch for a sachet.

Bag Pouch

Cut 2 pieces of fabric, each measuring 5″ × 3½″. Pin the pieces, right sides together; then stitch down the sides and across the bottom. Use regular machine stitch ½″ in from edges. Trim off the corners. See Figure III-6. Fold the top edge down ¼″, and press. Fold down another ¼″, and press. Pin, then machine stitch close to the edge or hem by hand. See Figure III-7.

Turn the pouch right side out and press. Fill to within about 1½″ of the top with a sachet mixture. Secure the top with a small elastic band. Tie a satin ribbon around the band in a bow. Add a small silk flower. See Figure III-8.

Figure III–8. A finished bag pouch for a sachet.

Decorating the Pouch

Pouches may be decorated with purchased appliqués, with tiny satin bows, with silk flowers, or with lace or eyelet trim. For lace or eyelet trim, purchase ready-made ½"- to 1"-wide ruffled trim—enough to go all around the pouch, with 1" to spare. Join the short ends of the trim, right sides together, with a ½" seam, using regular machine stitch. Press the seam open.

Pin the trim to the front of the pouch, wrong side of trim to right side of pouch. Sew by hand, using blind stitch (refer to Figure I-6) or hem stitch (refer to Figure I-5). Use matching-colored thread.

Sachet Recipes

Most of these ingredients are readily available at supermarkets, health food stores, or drug stores.

The bulk of the mixture is made up of dried flower petals and leaves. Herbs and spices are used as blenders and to provide scent. Essential oils are used to enhance the existing scent, and a fixative is added to make the sachet long lasting.

In each of the recipes given below, simply toss together the ingredients named.

Lavender Sachet Ingredients (makes 8 to 10 sachets):
2 cups Lavender Flowers
A few drops Lavender Oil
½ oz Powdered Orrisroot

Rose Sachet Ingredients (makes 12 to 14 sachets):
2 cups Dried Rose Petals
1 cup Dried Rose-Geranium Leaves
A few drops Rose-Geranium Oil
½ oz Powdered Orrisroot

Mint Sachet Ingredients (makes about 12 sachets):
2 cups Dried Mint Leaves
½ cup Dried Rosemary Leaves
A few drops Peppermint Oil
½ oz Powdered Orrisroot

Lemon Sachet Ingredients (makes 12 to 14 sachets):
2 cups Dried Lemon Balm Leaves
1 cup Dried Lemon Verbena Leaves
1 tbsp Grated Lemon Peel
A few drops Lemon Verbena Oil
A few drops Lemon Scent
½ oz Powdered Orrisroot

Spice Sachet Ingredients (makes about 20 sachets):
1 cup Dried Rose Petals
1 cup Dried Orange Blossoms
1 cup Lavender Flowers
1½ tsp Dried Rosemary
1½ tsp Dried Nutmeg
1½ tsp Ground Cinnamon
1½ tsp Ground Cloves
1½ tsp Ground Allspice
1 tbsp Powdered Orrisroot

Orange-Spice Sachet Ingredients (makes 8 to 10 sachets):
2 cups Dried Orange Blossoms
1 tbsp Dried Orange Peel
1 tbsp Whole Cloves
A few drops Bergamot Oil
½ oz Powdered Orrisroot

Soap Wraps
(for Women's Soap Baskets)

Use fine net fabric (tulle); it can be bought in white and in colors. If you cannot find the color you want, consider dying the white net.

Cut out circles with 8" diameters, using pinking shears. You may of course make the circles smaller or larger, depending on the size of the soap.

Place the bar of soap in the center. Gather the net around the soap and secure it with a small elastic band. Tie a satin ribbon around the band in a bow. Tuck a tiny silk blossom in the band if you wish.

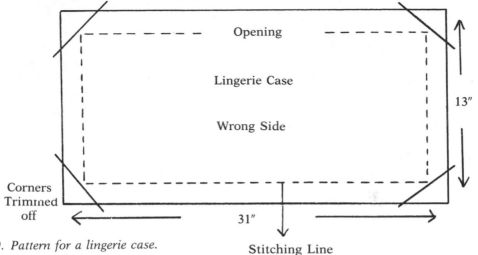

Figure III–9. Pattern for a lingerie case.

Lingerie Cases
(for Lingerie Organizer Baskets)

These cases can be made in any size. The pattern and method of sewing are very simple, so, if you wish to alter the size, you will have no problem. Choose such fabrics as satin, fine cotton, velvet, brocades, silk, and taffeta.

Each case takes only a small amount of fabric, so they are not expensive. You may even find remnants of costly fabrics at reasonable prices in fabric or fabric outlet stores.

Materials:
¾ yard of 36″-wide Fabric
Matching Thread
Embroidery Silk (six strand) in a Matching or
    Contrasting Color
Cut out a paper pattern as shown in Figure III-9. Next, cut out the pattern shape from fabric.

Place the fabric pieces right sides together, and pin. Stitch along both short ends and one long side. Stitch in 10″ from both ends on the remaining long side, leaving the center part open, as shown in Figure III-9.

Trim off the corners, turn the material right side out, and push out the corners with the tips of your scissors. Press, and then blind stitch across the opening (refer to Figure I-6).

Fold the bottom third of the rectangle up, and pin. See Figure III-10.

Using embroidery thread, work buttonhole stitch (see Figure III-11) or overstitch (refer to Figure I-8) around the sides and the top of the case. See Figure III-12.

Fold the top third of the case down over the "pocket" and mark the center or both corners for closings. Use press studs or Velcro circles.

The case may be decorated with purchased appliqués. Tuck a scented sachet in each finished case.

Figure III–10. Folding fabric to make a lingerie case.

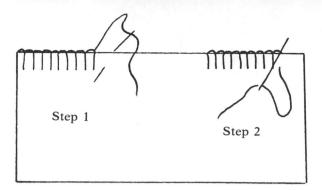

Figure III–11. Buttonhole stitch for a lingerie case.

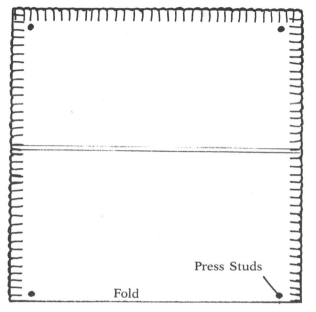

Press Studs

Fold

Figure III–12. Stitching a lingerie case.

Case Variations: Pouch

Cut 2 pieces of fabric, each measuring 13″ × 21″ (for lingerie cases), 16″ × 25″ (for sweater cases), or 12″ × 13″ (for pajama cases).

Construct as for a basic case. Fold the finished rectangle in half, and pin. Work buttonhole stitch or overstitch around the bottom and sides. If you wish, you can also work the same stitch around each single top edge. See Figure III-13.

Use press studs or Velcro circles sewn at three places along the top edge to keep the case closed.

Case Variations: Zippered Pouch

You will need a regular or invisible zipper that is the same size as the top edge of your finished pouch.

Make the case as above, omitting closures, and turn the case inside out. Open the zipper and place it along the top edges of the case, right side down. The bottom end of the zipper should be even with the side edge of the case. See Figure III-14. The zipper tabs will extend about 1″ at either end of the case. Pin the zipper in place. Hand stitch along each side of the zipper close to the teeth, using backstitch (see Figure III-15). Turn the case right side out and close the zipper.

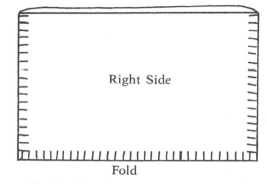

Right Side

Fold

Figure III–13. Lingerie case variations: Pouch.

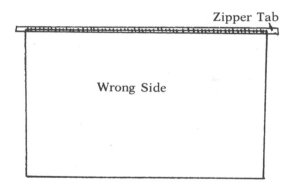

Zipper Tab

Wrong Side

Figure III–14. Lingerie case variations: Zippered pouch.

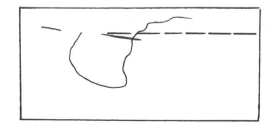

Figure III–15. Backstitch for a zippered pouch.

Case Variations: Ribboned Pouch

Cut out the pattern as for a plain pouch. Before sewing the pieces together, cut 4 lengths of 1"-wide satin ribbon, each 9" long, and place them on the right side of 1 piece of fabric as shown in Figure III-16. Baste across the ribbon ends on the seam line—½" in from edges. Place the second piece of fabric down over the ribboned piece, right sides together. Finish as for a plain pouch. When the pouch is completed, tie ribbons in bows at the top. See Figure III-17.

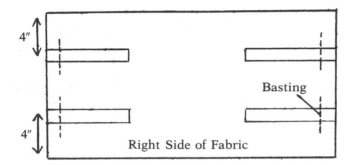

Figure III–16. Lingerie case variations: Ribboned pouch.

Figure III–17. A finished ribboned pouch.

Pajama Cases

Construct pajama cases the same way lingerie cases are made, only increase the pattern size to 16" × 37".

Use the same types of fabric given for lingerie cases. Children's cases can be made from fabric especially designed for children or from felt.

The back of the finished pajama case can be trimmed with a lace or eyelet ruffle, 2"–2½" wide. Make and attach the trim as for a trimmed sachet pouch (page 73).

Purchased appliqués, satin bows, or velvet ribbon may also be used for decoration.

The back of the case will now become the front, with the opening to the back. It can be placed on top of the bed as a "pillow."

Sweater Cases

Make sweater cases the same way lingerie cases are made, only increase the pattern size to 16" × 37".

These cases do not need to be trimmed with fancy trimmings since they will be used mainly to store sweaters.

Tuck a scented sachet in each finished case.

Hosiery Cases

Make hosiery cases the same way lingerie cases are made, only decrease the pattern size to 12" × 28". If you want to make a pouch-type case, cut the pattern at 12" × 19".

Bath Mat
(for Women's, Men's, or Children's Bath Baskets)

This attractive, absorbent mat will be a welcome part of any bath basket.

Materials:
¾ yard of 36"-wide Terrycloth or Cotton Fabric
1 yard Preshrunk Fringe
Matching Thread

Cut the pattern as shown in Figure III-18, first out of paper, then out of fabric. Cut the fringe into 2 lengths, each measuring 16".

On 1 piece of fabric, on the right side, place the fringes along both ends as shown in Figure III-19. Have the edge of the fringe even with the edge of the fabric, and pin in place. Baste the fringe to the fabric along the seam line—$\frac{1}{2}$" in from edges. Place the second piece of fabric over the fringed piece, right sides together, and pin. Stitch all around the mat, $\frac{1}{2}$" in from the edges, leaving open 6" along one long side. Use regular machine stitch. Trim off the corners, then turn mat right side out. Push out the corners gently with the tips of your scissors and press the mat. Blind stitch (refer to Figure I-6) across the opening.

Bath or Beach Pillow
(for Women's or Men's Bath Baskets or for Beach Baskets)

A bath pillow makes a unique and thoughtful gift. Inveterate readers will be especially delighted with one.

Materials:
$\frac{1}{2}$ yard of 36"-wide Terrycloth or Cotton Fabric
$\frac{1}{2}$ yard Unbleached Muslin or Cotton
Matching Thread
$1\frac{1}{2}$ lbs Foam Chips for Stuffing

Cut 1 pattern for the fabric outer pillow and 1 pattern for the muslin inner pillow. See Figure III-20.

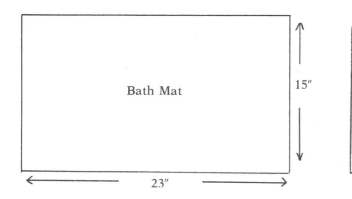

Figure III–18. Pattern for a bath mat.

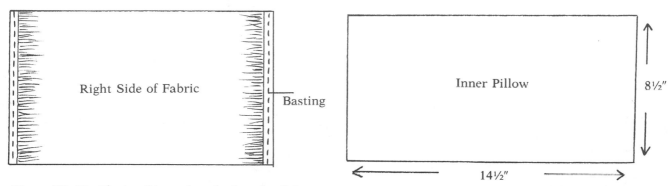

Figure III–19. Placing fringe along both ends of the bath mat.

Figure III–20. Pattern for a bath pillow.

Bath Mitt

Actual Size

Inner Pillow

Place the muslin pieces together, and pin. Stitch all around, using regular machine stitch, ½" in from the edges, leaving a 4" opening along 1 side. Trim off the corners and turn the material right side out. Stuff with foam chips (be generous when stuffing), and then blind stitch across the opening.

Outer Pillow

Make this the same way as you would the inner pillow, but increase the opening to 8". Place the inner pillow inside the outer pillow and blind stitch across opening.

Bath Mitt
(for Women's, Men's, or Children's Bath Baskets)

Materials
½ yard of 36"-wide Terrycloth Fabric
Matching Thread

First make the paper pattern, then cut the pattern shape out of the fabric. See Figure III-21.

Pin 2 pieces of fabric, right sides together, and stitch around the mitt, ½" in from the edges, leaving the top open. Trim the seam to ¼", then turn the mitt right side out. Turn the top edge in ½", and press.

Stitch the other 2 pieces of fabric together the same way, but do not turn them right side out. Turn the top down ½", and press.

Place one mitt inside the other, wrong sides together. Blind stitch around the top edge.

Herb Bags
(for Women's Bath Baskets)

Start with fine net fabric. Using pinking shears, cut out circles with 6" diameters.

Pile 1 or 2 tbsp of herbs in the center of each circle and gather the fabric as for the gathered

Figure III–21. Pattern for a bath mitt.

pouch on page 71. Tie an 18" piece of ribbon around the center of the bag, leaving the ends loose. The bag can be tied over a tap so that water can flow through it. It can also be steeped like tea, and the liquid added to bath water.

Herbs You Might Include:

Rosemary	Lemon Balm
Mint	Basil
Camomile	Lavender
Scented Geranium	Swiss Kriss

Tablecloth
(for Picnic and Dining Table Baskets)

A tablecloth is easy to make from a bedsheet. There is no need for center seams—the cloth can be cut from a single piece of fabric.

You can find many lovely patterns among bedsheets, and you can save money if you watch for sales.

Materials:
1 Single Flat Bedsheet
Matching Thread
7 yards of 2½"–3"-wide Fringe (optional)

Make a paper pattern, then cut the pattern shape from the fabric. See Figure III-22.

Turn under ½" all around the fabric piece, and press. Turn under another ½", and press. Miter the corners (see Figure III-23) and pin all around to secure.

Machine stitch close to the edge, or hand hem. Blind stitch along the corner seam.

Optional Fringe

Measure all around the cloth and then cut enough fringe to fit the circumference, with 1" to spare. Join the fringe, right sides together, at the short ends, with a ½" seam, to form a continuous strip. Press the seam open. Pin the fringe to the right side of the tablecloth, and stitch by machine or hand. Alternatively, the edge of the fringe may be sewn to the underside of the cloth.

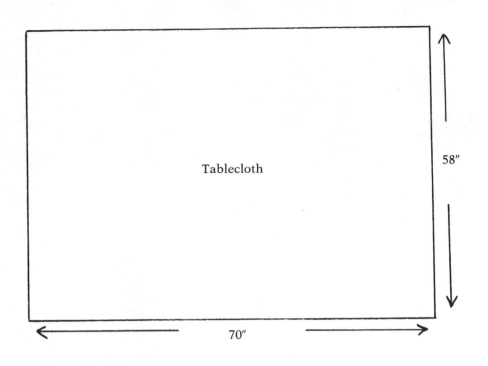

Figure III–22. Pattern for a tablecloth.

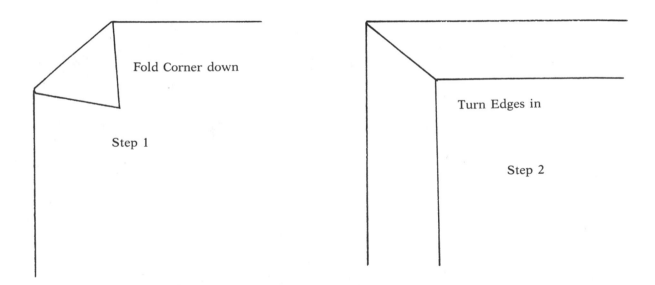

Figure III–23. Tablecloth: Miter the corners and pin all around to secure.

Napkins

(for Picnic and Dining Table Baskets)

Cloth napkins impart a tone of quiet elegance to a meal that everyone will appreciate.

Materials:
¾ yard of 36″-wide Drip-Dry Cotton Fabric
Matching Thread

Cut a paper pattern measuring 13″ × 13″, then cut the pattern shape from the fabric. You will get 4 napkins from the above yardage.

The napkins are sewn the same way as the tablecloth is, but omitting the fringe. Purchased appliqués may be sewn at one corner of each napkin for that little extra touch.

Napkin Holders

(for Picnic and Dining Table Baskets)

Napkin holders make a nice addition to any dining table, and they are so easy to make.

Decorated Wooden Holders

Attach a silk blossom to a plain wooden napkin holder with a drop of white glue. That's all there is to it—it makes a lovely napkin ring.

Fabric Strip

Tiny pieces of fabric are all you will need to make these easy holders. Use scraps left over from making the tablecloth or napkins.

First, make a paper pattern as shown in Figure III-24. Cut the pattern shape from the fabric and pin the fabric pieces, right sides together. Stitch all around, ½″ in from the edges, leaving a 2″ opening along one side of the material. Trim off the corners, and turn the material right side out. Push out the corners gently with the tips of your scissors, and press. Blind stitch across the opening. Press again, using spray starch to stiffen the holder. Sew a press stud at the end to keep the holder closed.

A tiny appliqué or silk flower can be sewn in the center of the holder or over the closing point.

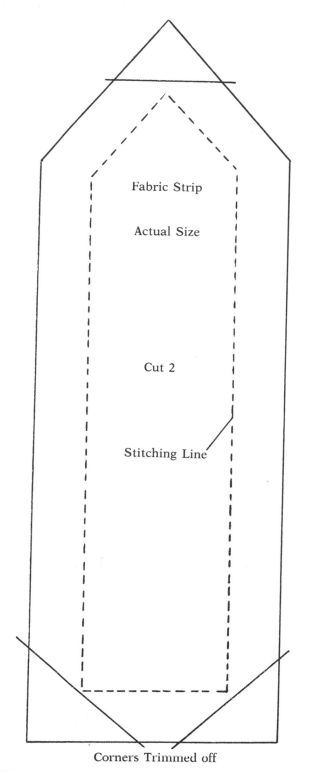

Figure III–24. Pattern for the fabric strip for a napkin holder.

Fabric Diamond

Cut 2 pieces of fabric, each measuring 5″ × 5″, place the pieces right sides together, and pin. Stitch all around the holder, $\frac{1}{2}$″ in from edges, leaving a 2″ opening along one side. Trim off the corners, and turn the material right side out. Blind stitch across the opening, and press, using starch. Fold the holder as shown in Figure III-25. Take a few stitches through all thicknesses to secure or sew a press stud at the closing point. Decorate the front of the holder with a silk flower.

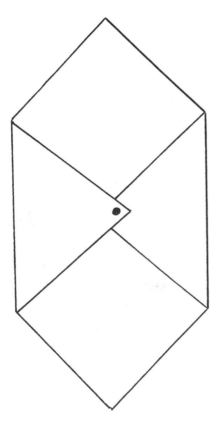

Figure III–25. A diamond napkin holder made of fabric.

Cutlery Holder
(for Picnic Baskets)

Cut 2 pieces of fabric, each measuring $10\frac{1}{2}$″ × 11″. On 1 piece of fabric cut three slits as shown in Figure III-26. Work buttonhole stitch (refer to Figure III-11) around the slits. Cut 4 pieces of felt or fabric, each measuring $5\frac{1}{2}$″ × $1\frac{1}{2}$″. Position the felt on back of the fabric so that the top edge of the felt strip is 1″ above the slit and the bottom edge is even with the edge of the fabric. Stitch all around the felt, $\frac{1}{4}$″ in from the edges.

On the right side of the same piece of fabric, place a 14″ piece of ribbon folded in half as shown in Figure III-27. Baste across the seam line, $\frac{1}{2}$″ in from the edge.

Place the second piece of fabric over the first piece, right sides together, and pin. Stitch all around the holder, $\frac{1}{2}$″ in from the edges, leaving open 4″ along one long side. Trim off the corners and turn the holder right side out. Push out the corners with the tips of your scissors. Blind stitch across the opening, and press. The handles of a knife, a fork, and a spoon are slipped into the tiny openings, the holder is rolled up, and the ribbon is tied around it in a bow. See Figure III-28.

Wash Mitt
(for Car Care Baskets)

Make the wash mitt as you would a bath mitt, but cut the pattern 2″ longer. Cut both the mitt and the lining from terrycloth fabric.

Polishing Mitt
(for Car Care Baskets)

Use the same pattern and fabric amount as for a bath mitt (page 79). Purchase washable fake fur fabric with a fairly long pile for the mitt, and for the lining choose a polyester and cotton blend.

Lay the pattern on back of the fur fabric and pin it in place. Use a sharp razor blade to slice through the backing of the fabric only—try not to cut the pile. Place the 2 pieces right side together, and pin. Make sure there are no fibers caught in the seam. Machine stitch all around the mitt, $\frac{1}{4}$" in from edges, or overstitch by hand. Leave the top of the mitt open. Turn the mitt right side out and use a toothpick to pry out any fibers caught in the seam. Turn the top edge in $\frac{1}{2}$", and pin.

Make the lining the same way, except don't turn it right side out. Turn down the top edge of the lining $\frac{1}{2}$", and press. Slip the lining into the mitt and blind stitch it in place, after removing the pins from the mitt, across the edges.

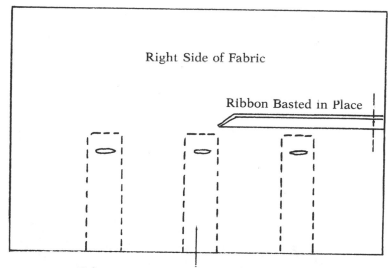

Figure III–26. Cutlery holder: On one piece of fabric, cut three slits.

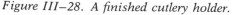

Figure III–27. On the right side of the same piece of fabric, place the ribbon.

Figure III–28. A finished cutlery holder.

Pet Cushion
(for Pet Care Baskets)

This cushion is made to fit in the bottom of the basket, turning the basket into a bed for someone's favorite pet.

Materials:
Fabric
Unbleached Muslin or Cotton
Matching Thread
Stuffing (old clean stockings, lint from your dryer,
    fabric scraps, purchased stuffing)

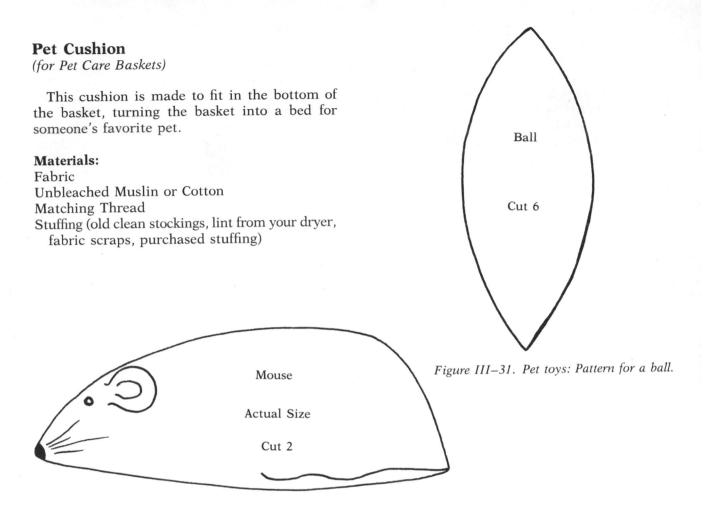

Ball

Cut 6

Figure III–31. Pet toys: Pattern for a ball.

Mouse

Actual Size

Cut 2

Figure III–29. Pet toys: Pattern for a toy mouse.

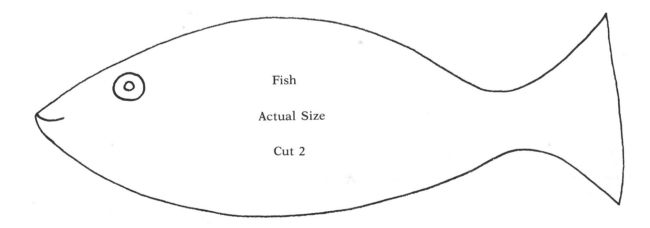

Fish

Actual Size

Cut 2

Figure III–30. Pet toys: Pattern for a toy fish.

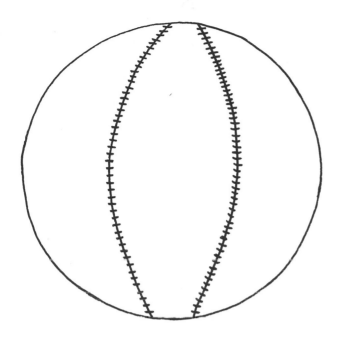

Figure III–32. A finished ball.

Measure the bottom of the basket and add ½" all around. Cut out a paper pattern. Cut out 2 pieces of fabric, using this pattern. Next, cut off ¼" from all around the paper pattern. Cut out 2 pieces of muslin, using this smaller pattern.

Make the pillow the same way the bath pillow is constructed (see page 77). You may sprinkle some catnip over the stuffing if the pillow is for a cat.

If you wish to, you can eliminate the inner pillow and stuff the outer cover. If you do this, though, remember that there will be no cover to take off and wash when it becomes necessary.

Pet Toys
(for Pet Care Baskets)

Use felt to make these simple little toys, and mark facial features with nontoxic marker pens.

Cut a paper pattern from Figure III-29 or Figure III-30. Place the pieces of felt together, and pin. Machine stitch all around or overstitch the edges by hand. Leave a small, 1½" opening along one edge. Stuff with your chosen stuffing and sew up the opening. Catnip may be sprinkled inside toys for cats.

For a ball, cut a pattern from Figure III-31. Place 2 pieces of felt together and overstitch them along one side. Open up the piece and attach another piece of felt the same way. See Figure III-32. Continue in this way until all the felt pieces have been joined. Before sewing the last seam to form the ball, stuff firmly with your chosen stuffing.

Cloth Doll
(for Doll Baskets)

Cut a paper pattern of a doll from Figures III-33, III-34, and III-35.

Materials:
¼ yard of 36"-wide Cotton, Flannel, or Cotton Knit Fabric (flesh-colored, pink, or white)
Matching Thread
Stuffing
1 skein Double Knit Wool
Embroidery Silk (small pieces—red, black, and blue)

Cut the fabric using the pattern. Pin the body pieces, right sides together. Stitch all around ½" in from the edges, leaving the bottom open. Turn the material right side out. Turn in ½" along the bottom edge, and press. Stuff the body firmly, then blind stitch or overstitch across the opening.

Pin 2 of the arm sections, right sides together. Stitch all around, ½" in from edges, leaving the shoulder end open. Repeat with the other 2 arm sections. Turn the material right side out, and stuff. Turn in ½" at the shoulder end and sew as for the bottom of the body. Overstitch each arm to the body, positioning each so that the top of the arm is even with the top of the shoulder on the body part.

Construct the legs in the same way you did the arms. Sew to the body section as above, having the side of the legs even with the side of the body. See Figure III-36.

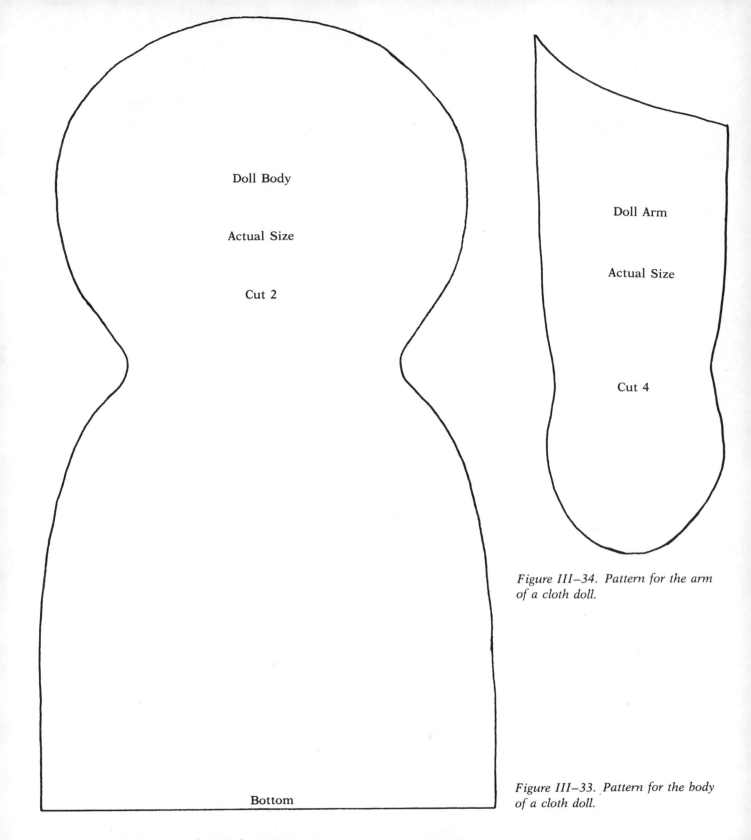

Doll Body

Actual Size

Cut 2

Bottom

Doll Arm

Actual Size

Cut 4

Figure III–34. Pattern for the arm of a cloth doll.

Figure III–33. Pattern for the body of a cloth doll.

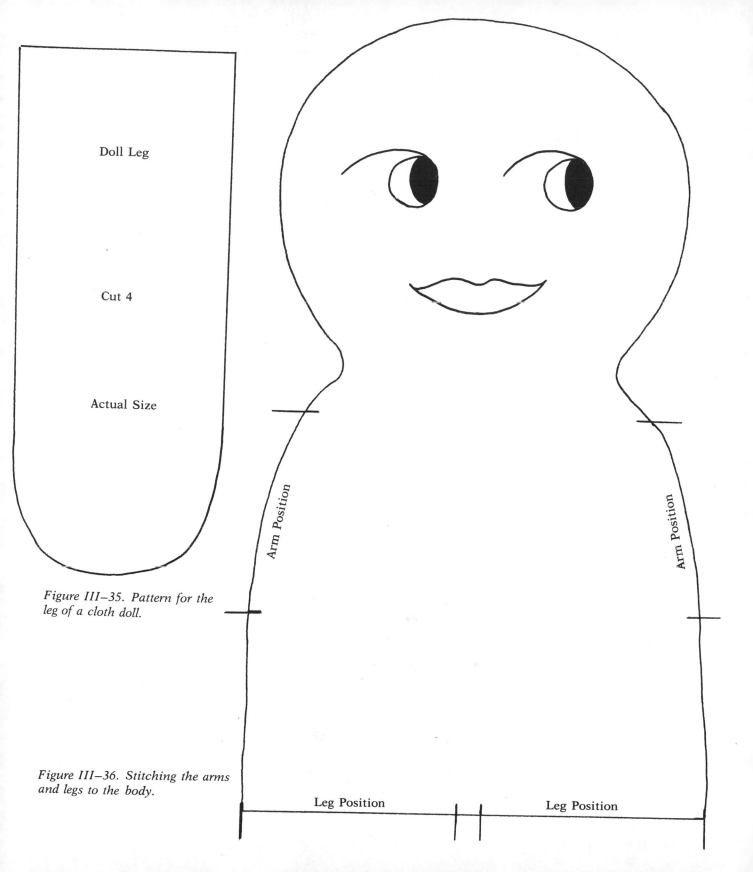

Doll Leg

Cut 4

Actual Size

Figure III–35. Pattern for the leg of a cloth doll.

Arm Position

Arm Position

Figure III–36. Stitching the arms and legs to the body.

Leg Position

Leg Position

Hair

Wind the wool around a 9" piece of cardboard, then cut it along one end. Take about 30 strands of the wool and place them side by side on a 4" × ½" piece of fabric or felt so that 2" overlaps the edge of the felt. Stitch the wool to the felt by machine or by hand. See Figure III-37. Stitch the felt to the doll's head, with the short end of the fringe falling over the forehead of the doll.

Spread the rest of the wool evenly across a 4" × ½" piece of felt so that the felt is at the center of the wool. See Figure III-38. Stitch the wool to the felt as before. Turn the edges of felt under and secure them with a few small stitches. Place the felt strip down the back of the doll head and stitch it in place using backstitch (refer to Figure III-15). Divide the wool at the neckline and tie each side with ribbons. Cut the fringe to just above the eyebrows.

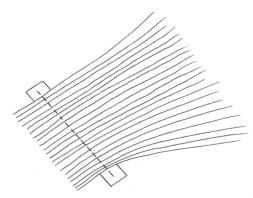

Figure III–37. Stitching wool to felt for the doll's hair.

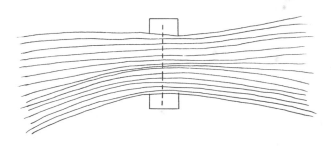

Figure III–38. Stitching the doll's hair: Spread the wool across a 4" × ½" piece of felt. Position the felt at the center of the wool.

Face

Using black embroidery thread, work the eyebrows in stem stitch (see Figure III-39). Eyes and mouth are worked in satin stitch (see Figure III-40), in blue and red thread. If you wish, you can use nontoxic marker pens for the facial features.

Figure III–39. Stem stitch for the eyebrows of a cloth doll.

Figure III–40. Satin stitch for the eyes and mouth of a cloth doll.

Nightgown

Cut the paper pattern. Cut the pattern shape from the fabric. A small scrap of fabric is all you will need, plus about ½ yard of ½"-wide lace trim.

Place the pattern pieces right sides together, and pin. Stitch all around the neck and down both back edges. Use ½" seams and regular machine stitch. Trim off the corners and clip around the neck edge down to the stitching line every ½". See Figure III-41. Turn the material right side out, and press. Pin, and then stitch, using basting stitch, around the entire outer edge of the nightgown. Fold the nightgown in half and stitch the underarm and side seams ½" in from the edges. Turn the material right side out, and press. Turn under ¼" along the bottom and sleeves, and press. Turn under another ¼", and pin. Hand hem it in place. Trim the bottom of the nightgown, the edge of the sleeves, and the edge of the neck with lace trim, if you wish. Sew a press stud or hook and eye at the top of the nightgown.

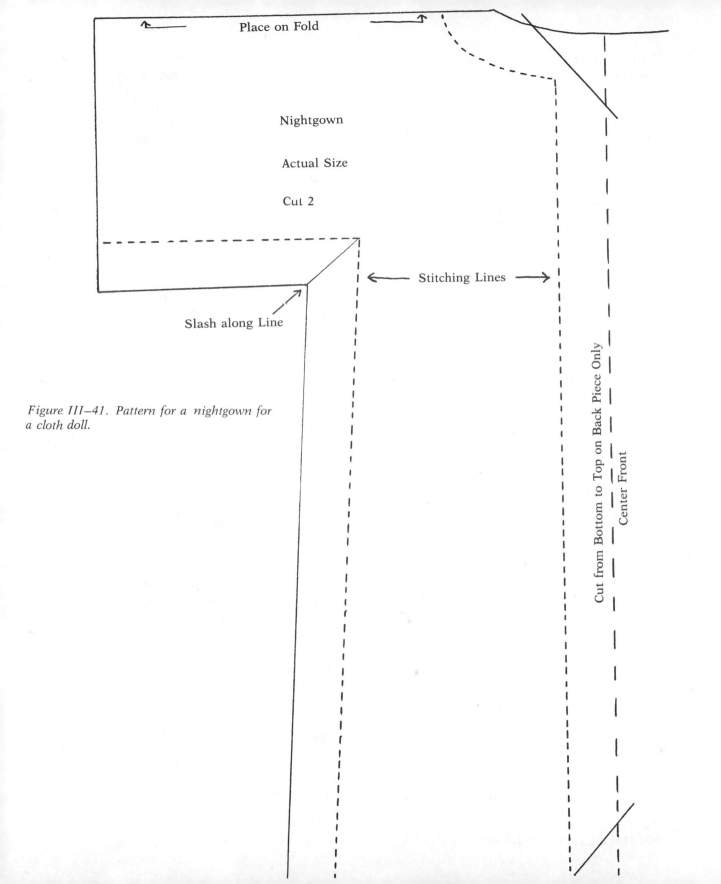

Place on Fold

Nightgown

Actual Size

Cut 2

Stitching Lines

Slash along Line

Figure III–41. Pattern for a nightgown for a cloth doll.

Cut from Bottom to Top on Back Piece Only

Center Front

Doll's Bedding
(for Doll Baskets)

Mattress

Use plain white cotton fabric. First, measure the size of the basket bottom and add ½″ all around. Cut 2 pieces of cotton with these measurements. Join the pieces, right sides together, with ½″ seams. Leave open 4″ along one side. Trim off the corners and turn the material right side out. Stuff the mattress with your chosen stuffing, and then blind stitch across the opening.

Pillow

Cut the pattern so that it is the same width as the basket, plus 1″, and about ¼ the length of the mattress. Join and sew as you did the mattress, leaving open 2″ instead of 4″. Stuff and finish as you did the mattress.

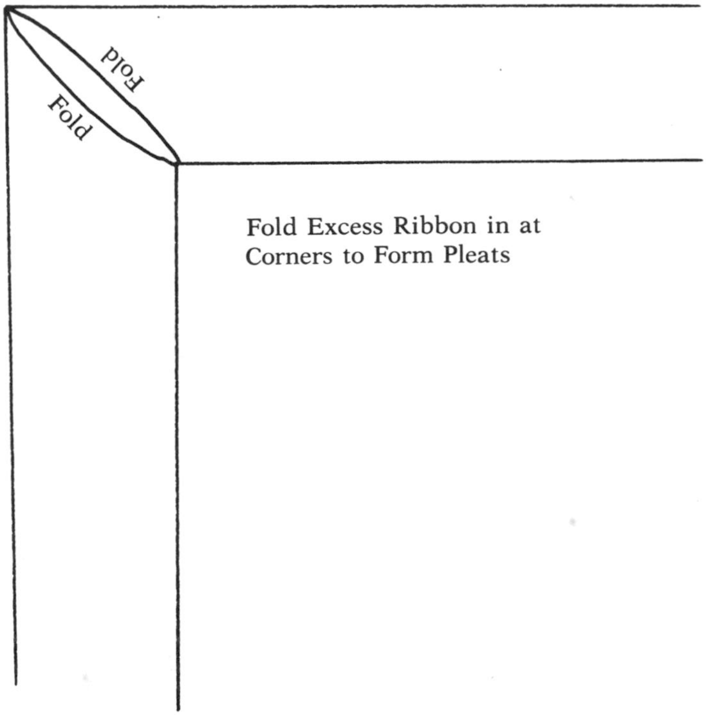

Fold

Fold

Fold Excess Ribbon in at
Corners to Form Pleats

Figure III–42. Making a blanket for a cloth doll.

Sheet

Cut a piece of white cotton that is 4½″ wider and 7″ longer than the mattress. Turn under ¼″ all around, and press. Turn under another ¼″, and pin. Miter the corners (refer to Figure III-23). Machine stitch all around, close to the edge, or hand hem.

Pillow Case

Cut 2 pieces of cotton, each 1½″ wider and 2″ longer than the pillow. Place the pieces right sides together, and pin. Stitch across the bottom and along the sides, leaving the top open. Use ½″ seams. Trim off the corners, turn the material right side out, and press. Turn in ¼″ at the top edges, and press. Turn in another ¼″, and pin. Machine sew around the edge or hand hem.

Blanket

Cut the blanket the same size as the finished sheet, from a small piece of flannel or an old blanket. Purchase enough 2″-wide satin ribbon to go all around the blanket, with 1″ to spare. Join the ribbon, right sides together, with a ½″ seam to form a continuous strip. Press the seam open. With the seam to the inside, fold the ribbon over the edge of the blanket, and pin. Make 2 small pleats in the ribbon at the corners. See Figure III-42. Stitch all around, close to the edges of the ribbon, and press.

Bedspread

Bedspreads look lovely when made from gaily colored cotton or gingham checks. You can trim the bedspread with an eyelet ruffle (purchase enough to go all around the spread, plus 1″).

For the bedspread, cut 2 pieces of fabric, each the same size as the sheet. Join the ruffle at its short ends, right sides together, and pin. Stitch with a ½″ seam to form a continuous strip. Press the seam open.

Pin the ruffle around the edge of one piece of the fabric, right sides together, with the edges of the frill even with the edges of the fabric. Baste it in place. Place the second piece of fabric over the frilled piece, right sides together, and pin. Stitch all around, ½″ in from the edges, leaving

4″ open along one side. Trim off the corners, turn the material right side out, and press. Blind stitch across the opening.

Egg Cozies
(for Dining Table Baskets)

A hot cooked egg on a cold morning is assured with a homemade egg cozy.

Materials:
Small Fabric Scraps
Quilt Batting
Plain Cotton (for lining)
Matching Thread

Cut the pattern according to Figure III-43. On the wrong side of each piece of fabric, place a piece of batting and a piece of lining so that the top edges are even. Pin them in place. Baste all around, ½″ in from the edges, leaving the bottom open. Place the padded pieces right sides together, and pin. Stitch all around, ½″ in from the edges, leaving the bottom open. Turn the material right side out. Turn in ¼″ at the bottom, and press. Turn up the rest of fabric over the padding, and pin. Hem it by hand.

Tab (optional)
Cut a piece of fabric 1″ × 3″. Fold it in half lengthwise, right sides together. Stitch all along the long side, ½″ in from the edge. Turn the material right side out. Stuff the tab with a little bit of quilt batting to within ½″ of the ends. Fold the tab in half and baste it to the top of one piece of the cozy, before sewing them together. See Figure III-44.

The cozy may be piped along the seam with purchased or homemade piping. To make your own piping, see page 22. Baste the piping to one side of the padded piece before sewing them together. See Figure III-45.

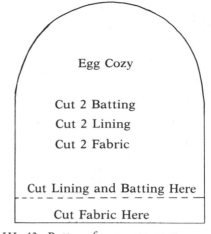

Figure III–43. Pattern for an egg cozy.

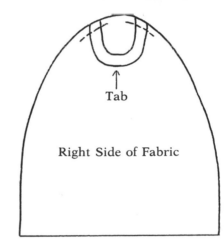

Figure III–44. Tab for an egg cozy.

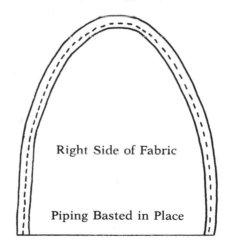

Figure III–45. Piping for an egg cozy.

Place Mats
(for Dining Table Baskets)

Cut 2 pieces of fabric, each measuring 15″ × 12″, for each mat. Place the pieces right sides together, and pin. Stitch all around, ½″ in from the edges, leaving a 4″ opening along one side. Trim off the corners and turn the material right side out. Press, and blind stitch across the opening.

The mat may be decorated by having purchased appliqués sewn at one corner.

Tea Cozy
(for Dining Table Baskets)

To keep an entire pot of tea warm at a meal or social gathering, this cozy does the job.

Materials:
2 pieces of 11″ × 10″ Fabric
2 pieces of 11″ × 10″ Quilt Batting
2 pieces of 11″ × 10″ Cotton
Matching Thread

Make the tea cozy using the same steps you would use for the egg cozy. Include piping and a tab if you wish. The pattern of the tea cozy is given in Figure III-46.

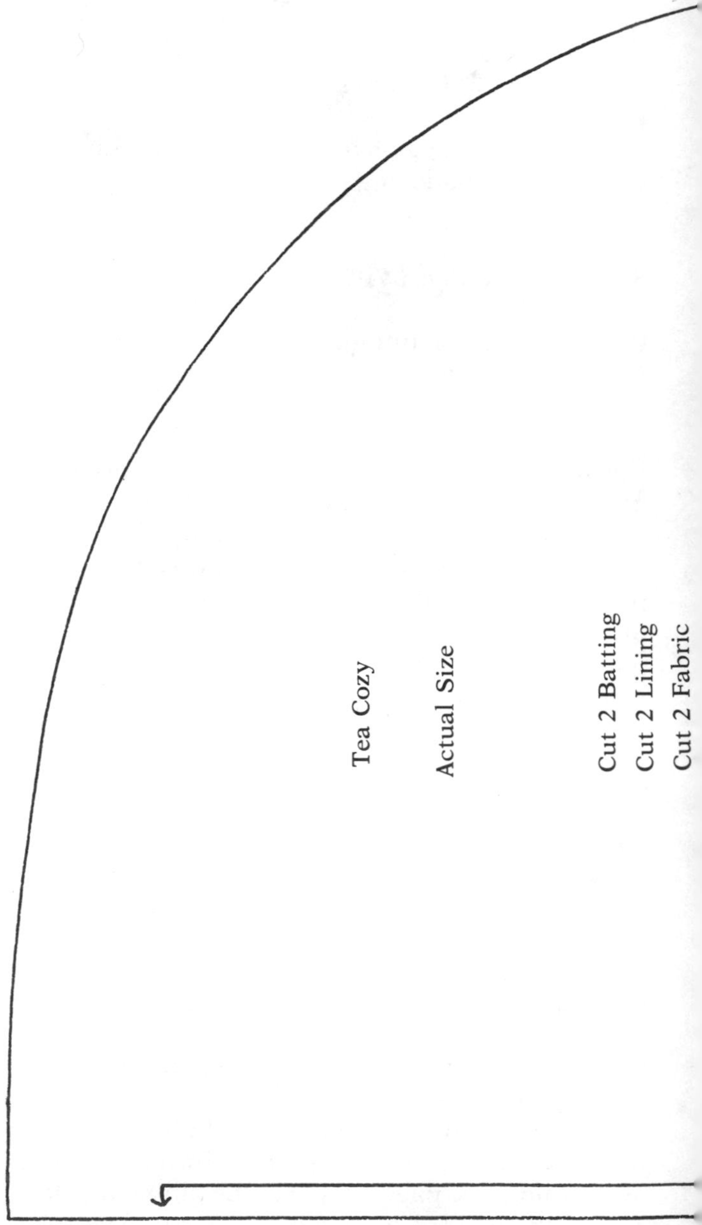

Figure III–46. Pattern for a tea cozy.

Tea Cozy

Actual Size

Cut 2 Batting
Cut 2 Lining
Cut 2 Fabric

Cut Lining and Batting Here

Cut Fabric Here

Place on Fold of Fabric

Metric Conversion Table

METRIC CONVERSION

to convert	to	multiply by
inches	centimeters	2.54
feet	meters	0.3048
yards	meters	0.9144
ounces	grams	28.35

The following are not *exact* measurements, but close equivalents, for your convenience.

VOLUMES

for	use
$\frac{1}{4}$ tsp	1ml
$\frac{1}{2}$ tsp	2ml
1 tsp	5ml
1 tbsp	15ml
1 cup	250ml
2 cups	500ml
1 ounce	30ml

LENGTHS

for	use
$\frac{1}{4}$ inch	0.6cm
$\frac{1}{2}$ inch	1.2cm
1 inch	2.5cm
1 foot	31cm
1 yard	1 meter

FABRIC WIDTHS

for	use
36 inches	90cm
45 inches	115cm
54 inches	140cm
60 inches	150cm

Index